D1605558

The Exile and Biblical Narrative

HARVARD SEMITIC MUSEUM

HARVARD SEMITIC MONOGRAPHS

edited by
Frank Moore Cross, Jr.

Number 22

THE EXILE AND BIBLICAL NARRATIVE
**The Formation of the Deuteronomistic
and Priestly Works**
by
Richard Elliott Friedman

Richard Elliott Friedman
THE EXILE
AND BIBLICAL
NARRATIVE
*The Formation of the Deuteronomistic
and Priestly Works*

Scholars Press

Distributed by
Scholars Press
PO Box 2268
Chico, California 95927

THE EXILE AND BIBLICAL NARRATIVE
*The Formation of the Deuteronomistic
and Priestly Works*

Richard Elliott Friedman

BS
1181.17
.F74

Portions of this volume appeared in other publications and are reprinted here with permission: "The Tabernacle in the Temple," in *Biblical Archaeologist 43* (1980). "From Egypt to Egypt: Dtr[1] and Dtr[2]," in *Traditions in Transformation: Turning-Points in Biblical Faith*, The Frank Moore Cross *Festschrift* (Eisenbrauns, 1980), B. Halpern and J. Levenson, eds.

Library of Congress Cataloging in Publication Data

Friedman, Richard E
    The exile and Biblical narrative.

    (Harvard Semitic monographs ; no. 22)
    Bibliography: p.
    1. D document (Biblical criticism)
2. P document (Biblical criticism) 3. Bible.
O.T.—Criticism, interpretation, etc. I. Title.
II. Series.
BS1181.17.F74   222'.1044   80-28836
ISBN 0-89130-457-6

This book is respectfully dedicated to my father

Alex Sandor Friedman

זכרונו לברכה

Table of Contents

Priestly Tabernacle Illustrations

Abbreviations

ASTI	*Annual of the Swedish Theological Institute*
BA	*The Biblical Archeologist*
BAR	*The Biblical Archeologist Reader*
CBQ	*Catholic Biblical Quarterly*
CMHE	Frank Moore Cross, *Canaanite Myth and Hebrew Epic*
DDS	Moshe Weinfeld, *Deuteronomy and the Deuteronomic School*
HAR	*Hebrew Annual Review*
HPT	Martin Noth, *A History of Pentateuchal Traditions*
HTR	*Harvard Theological Review*
HUCA	*Hebrew Union College Annual*
ILOT	S.R. Driver, *Introduction to the Literature of the Old Testament*
JAOS	*Journal of the American Oriental Society*
JBL	*Journal of Biblical Literature*
JNES	*Journal of Near Eastern Studies*
JQR	*Jewish Quarterly Review*
PHI	Julius Wellhausen, *Prolegomena to the History of Israel*
RB	*Revue Biblique*
RI	Yehezkel Kaufmann, *The Religion of Israel*
UGS	Martin Noth, *Überlieferungsgeschichtliche Studien*
VT	*Vetus Testamentum*
ZAW	*Zeitschrift für die alttestamentliche Wissenschaft*

Chapter I

The Impact of Exile on the Character
of the Deuteronomistic History

I. That there were two editions of the Deuteronomistic history, the first Josianic, the second Exilic.

The many and various scholarly conceptions of numerous redactions of numerous sources of the *n^{e}bî'îm ri'šōnîm* (the books of Joshua, Judges, Samuel, and Kings) came to a welcome demise with the arrival of Martin Noth's *Überlieferungsgeschichtliche Studien.*[1] Noth saw these books not as an assemblage but as a work, the task of a single person, a writer/editor with a particular perspective and intention. That person selected source materials and wrote passages at all times developing this perspective, occasionally referring the reader back to the sources for data which did not serve the writer/editor's interest.[2] This tradent thus told, in *n^{e}bî'îm ri'šōnîm*, a continuing story of the people of Israel from the era of their arrival in a new land to the time of their forced exile in Babylonia. The speeches of important figures in the story, together with judgmental remarks of the tradent, crystallized the fact that these books were not annals but rather a directed historical account. The key to the perspective of this directed history was the old core of the book of Deuteronomy together with a newly added introduction and conclusion[3] which suited the book's new role as platform and *Leitmotif* of a history. The full work thus told Israel's story from Moses to the Davidid king Jehoiachin in Exile, attributing Israel's current homelessness to the centuries of failure of the people and its kings to fulfill that which had been demanded of them in Moses' book. Noth thus suitably spoke of the work as the Deuteronomistic history. He naturally regarded the author as an exile.

---

[1] Martin Noth, *Überlieferungsgeschichtliche Studien* (original edition 1943), (hereafter cited as *UGS*).

[2] Including the Chronicles of Solomon, the Chronicles of the Kings of Israel, and the Chronicles of the Kings of Judah.

[3] Deut. 1-3; 31:1ff.

2

Gerhard von Rad took special regard of a recurring theme which seemed to contradict this Deuteronomistic scheme of disaster as consequence of breach of the covenant demands of Deuteronomy.[4] This countertheme centered in the promise of YHWH to David of eternal security for David's dynasty and for David's city, Jerusalem. Justice and grace seemed to stand in an impossible tension. The resolution of this "theological dilemma," said von Rad, came when the word of judgment proved stronger than the word of grace in the day of Israel's calamity. The last four verses of the history, nonetheless, permitted a slight flickering of hope for a rekindling of grace through the person of Jehoiachin, recently released from prison by the Babylonian king (2 Kings 25:27-30).

Hans Walter Wolff emphasized another theme to which Noth had not done justice.[5] A theme of hope, albeit a small one, surfaced in short passages at key junctures in the Deuteronomistic history. This was not the hope in the Davidic dynasty, which von Rad had outlined. According to Wolff, the Deuteronomist had regrooved the tradition of an eternal promise to David by adding conditions to the terms of the conveyance. The expression of the promise in 1 Kings 9:4f. for example was, in the Deuteronomist's full context (vv. 6-9), more a threat than a commitment. The hope which the Deuteronomist offered to the exiled Jews, said Wolff, lay not in the monarchy but in the people. The last speeches of Moses (Deut. 4:25-31; 30:1-20) and the Temple dedication prayer of Solomon (1 Kings 8:46-53) offered hope of restoration to an exiled nation who would turn back to YHWH in repentance.

While both these respective themes of von Rad and Wolff presented serious problems to Noth's understanding of the Deuteronomistic history, neither von Rad nor Wolff challenged Noth's primary contention that the work was a single Exilic tradent's product. They rather attempted to comprehend and reconcile the thematic conflicts with the interests of that tradent in Babylonia. Frank Moore Cross has regarded the theme of the eternal promise to the house of David as far more critical to our understanding of the Deuteronomistic history and of the editorial process which

---

[4] Gerhard von Rad, *Studies in Deuteronomy*, pp. 74-79. See also von Rad, *Old Testament Theology* I, pp. 334-347; "The Deuteronomic Theology of History in I and II Kings," in *The Problem of the Hexateuch*, pp. 205-221.

[5] Hans Walter Wolff, "Das Kerygma des deuteronomistischen Geschichtswerkes," *ZAW* 73 (1961), pp. 171-186.

produced it than von Rad suggested.[6] The co-existence of an account of a divine promise of a never ending kingdom with an account of the destruction and exile of that kingdom is more than a "theological dilemma." It is a crucial clue to uncovering a more complex literary process than Noth depicted. The Davidic dynastic promise is portrayed as such in only a few passages, but their import is patent. The initial declaration of the commitment to David, pronounced by the Prophet Nathan, is powerful:

> YHWH will make a House[7] for you. When your days will be full and you will lie with your fathers, I shall establish your seed, who will come from your insides, after you. He will build a house for my name, and I shall sustain the throne of his kingdom forever. I shall be a father to him, and he will be a son to me, whom I shall chastise with the rod of humans and the lashes of men when he does wrong, but my *hesed*[8] will not turn from him as I turned from Saul, whom I turned out from before you. Your house and your kingdom will be secure before you forever, your throne will be established forever.

2 Sam. 7:11b-16

The wording is clear and unequivocal. The prayer of David which follows (vv. 18-29) underlines the point, as do three later notations in the history of the dynasty. When the prophet Ahijah announces that the offenses of Solomon against YHWH are to result in forfeiture of reign over Israel to Jeroboam, he declares:

> But I shall not take the whole kingdom from his hand, for I shall make him a prince all the days of his life for the sake of David my servant whom I chose, who kept my commandments and laws. I shall take the kingdom from the hand of his son and give it to you — the ten tribes. But I shall give one tribe to his son so that there

---

[6] Frank Moore Cross, *Canaanite Myth and Hebrew Epic*, pp. 274-289, (hereafter cited as *CMHE*).

[7] Hebrew *bāyit*, refers to dynasty.

[8] The untranslatable *hesed* refers to the kindness shown in fidelity to a covenant relationship, almost always coming from the stronger of the covenant parties.

may be a fief[9] for my servant David always before me in
Jerusalem, the city which I have chosen for myself to ·
set my name there.

1 Kings 11:34-36

Despite the offenses of Solomon's successors, Rehoboam and
Abijah, YHWH continues to sustain the throne in Jerusalem
because of the merit of David. Abijah

> went in all the crimes of his father which he had done
> before him, and his heart was not whole[10] with YHWH
> his God as the heart of David his father. But for the
> sake of David YHWH his God gave him a fief in
> Jerusalem to establish his son after him and to establish
> Jerusalem.

1 Kings 15:3f

The Davidid Jehoram likewise receives undeserved divine protection on David's account.

> He went in the path of the kings of Israel . . . and he did
> evil in the eyes of YHWH, but YHWH was not willing
> to destroy Judah for the sake of David his servant, as he
> had promised him to give a fief to him and to his son
> always.

2 Kings 8:18f.

The equation to the kings of the Northern kingdom here is of
particular interest. Cross notes that the theme of the Davidic
promise in Judah is balanced against the ongoing theme of the
crimes of Jeroboam and his successors in Israel. Even when the

---

[9] On the meaning of the term nîr, see Paul Hanson, "Song of Heshbon and David's
NÎR," *HTR* 61 (1968), pp. 297-320.

[10] For examples of *whole heart* as covenant fidelity terminology, cf. the treaties:
Mursilis II of Hatti and Niqmepa of Ugarit, line 20, J. Nougayrol, *Palais royal
d'Ugarit* IV, pp. 84ff. (RS 17.353); Ashurnirari V and Mat'ilu of Bit-Agusi, Col. IV,
line 3, E. Weidner, *Archiv für Orientforschung* 8, 16ff., also in D.J. McCarthy, *Treaty
and Covenant*, p. 195; Essarhaddon's Vassal Treaty, lines 53, 387, in McCarthy,
Treaty and Covenant, p. 199. See also Moshe Weinfeld, "The Covenant of Grant in
the Old Testament and in the Ancient Near East," *JAOS* 90 (1970), pp. 184-203.

Davidid commits the very crimes of his Northern peer, his kingdom is not condemned to the same fate as that of Israel. Judah, on the contrary, survives long past the destruction of Israel and, in Josiah, seems to be entering upon a new golden age like that of David. Cross sees in this milieu the background of the first edition of the Deuteronomistic history. The paired themes of apostasy leading to destruction in the North and Davidic fidelity leading to preservation and ultimate restoration of the North to the Davidic line are precisely the interests of the Josianic reform. The two-and-a-half chapters which follow the Josiah pericope, according to Cross, are an updating of the history down to the time of Jehoiachin in Exile. Certain passages which seem to be addressed to exiles, together with passages which seem to soften the certainty of the Davidic promise, Cross attributes to the Exilic Deuteronomist (Dtr²) as well, including Deut. 4:27-31; 28;36f., 63-68; 29:27; 30:1-10; Josh. 23:11-13, 15f.; 1 Sam. 12:25; 1 Kings 2:4; 6:11-13; 8:25b, 46-53; 9:4-9; 2 Kings 17:19; 20:17f.; 21:2-15.

The remarkable consistency of the Deuteronomistic style and terminology has long been recognized as an overwhelming barrier to identification of plural hands in the work,[11] against which Cross has summoned literary and thematic evidence to support the notion of an original Josianic edition (Dtr¹) and a supplemental Exilic edition (Dtr²). Chief of these of course is the theme of the eternal maintenance of the kingdom, a rather strange theme for one to develop after 587. Cross also points to the notation of earlier literary critics that the expression "to this day" occurs regularly, often referring to circumstances which obtained only while the kingdom of Judah was still standing.[12] The matter of the re-acquisition of the North under Josiah seems likewise to be a datum which one would hardly expect an Exilic writer to emphasize so. The greater length of the narrative devoted to Josiah than to other Deuteronomistically-approved kings is another clue to be reckoned

---

[11] For a collection of Deuteronomistic phraseology, see Moshe Weinfeld, *Deuteronomy and the Deuteronomic School*, Appendix A, pp. 320-365, (hereafter cited as *DDS*). In the present work, the term "Deuteronomic" is used to refer exclusively to the book of Deuteronomy, as opposed to "Deuteronomistic," which applies to the entire Deuteronomistic history.

[12] 2 Kings 8:22; 16:6; see also 1 Kings 8:8; 9:21; 10:12; 12:19; 2 Kings 10:27; 14:7; 17:23.

with. Indeed, since the verdict for the destruction of the kingdom is traced to the crimes of Josiah's grandfather Manasseh (2 Kings 21:12-15; reckoned by Cross among the Dtr^2 insertions) the attention given to Josiah is a strange anticlimax. What one would expect to find, if the history were the work of a single Exilic tradent, would be a peroration on the fall of Jerusalem, comparable to that upon the destruction of the North (2 Kings 17:7-23). There is none. One might expect, as well, a concluding indicator of hope for restoration of the people to its land and a suggested repentance. There is none.

To these factors I would add certain changes in the fundamental perspective of the narrator which occur immediately following the Josiah narrative. Von Rad noted that the criterion by which the Deuteronomistic historian regularly evaluated the kings of Israel and Judah was their fulfillment or transgression of the requirement of centralization of worship. The Deuteronomist thus classified every one of the kings of Israel's two-century history as evil for having retained the alternate worship which Jeroboam had initiated at Dan and Bethel. The Deuteronomist likewise faulted all of the kings of Judah, except Hezekiah and Josiah, for having built or retained *bāmôt* outside the Jerusalem Temple. Hezekiah and Josiah draw the tradent's praise for having destroyed the *bāmôt*. Von Rad did not note, however, that in the account of the four kings who follow Josiah not a word about *bāmôt* appears, even though the *bāmôt* were revived in this period.[13] Why would an Exilic writer apply this criterion to every king except the four in whose reigns the calamities finally occurred?

Von Rad also noted a recurring prophecy/fulfillment pattern through the course of the Deuteronomistic history, pointing out eleven examples.[14] But this pattern likewise ceases after Josiah.

Another notable disappearance occurring after the Josiah pericope is that of David. Not only is the Davidic promise no longer an issue, but the regular rating of Judean kings in comparison to their father David ceases. Toward the end of the history one finds this family standard in the evaluation of Ahaz, Hezekiah, Manasseh, Amon (by implication) and Josiah, after which the criterion ceases.

---

[13] Cf. Jer. 17:3; Ezek. 6:3,6.

[14] Von Rad, "The Deuteronomic Theology," pp. 208-211.

These matters constitute more than arguments from silence. This is a full-fledged change of perspective and manner of presentation of history. The last four kings receive the shortest of ratings; they "did evil in the eyes of YHWH *according to all that their fathers had done*"—an unthoughtful choice of wording if the writer who described these kings was the same writer who had just described the career of their father Josiah.

Thus one can hardly view the emphasis upon Josiah as merely an Exilic author's perception of Josiah's activities as having been historically important. The literary evidence rather points to a full stop and subsequent addition. Josiah is more than important. His reign is the literary focus of the work. Josiah is the figure to whom the Deuteronomistic presentation of history is building. The prophecy of 1 Kings 13:2 which predicts him by name is, as Cross notes, a striking literary anticipation which particularly points to the Josianic perspective.

A remarkable series of associations between the Josiah account and the earliest portions of the Deuteronomist's story demonstrate the extent to which the depiction of Josiah was integral and climactic to the tradent's literary construction. The identification of the book of Deuteronomy, or a portion thereof, as the book found in the Temple during the reign of Josiah is as old as deWette and has been generally accepted since his time. A number of matters in Deuteronomy relate to the Josiah pericope in 2 Kings 22 and 23 both in theme and phraseology.

The closing reference to Moses following his death in Deuteronomy commences with the words, "There did not arise a prophet again in Israel like Moses. . ." (*l' qm nby' ʿwd byśr'l kmšh*) Deut. 34:10. This precise expression, "none arose like him," is not applied to any other Biblical personage but one. The closing reference to Josiah following the account of his reform reads, "There was no king like him before him turning to YHWH with all his heart and with all his soul and with all his might according to all the Torah of Moses, and after him none arose like him," (2 Kings 23:25).[15] The parallel occurrence of the phrase appears to be more than a chance colloquy when one notes that a second parallel occurs in the same verse. The well-known command of Deut. 6:5, "Love YHWH your God with all your heart and with all your soul and

---

[15] Jack R. Lundbom, "The Lawbook of the Josianic Reform," *CBQ* 38 (1976) notes this parallel, pp. 301f.

8

with all your might," appears in precisely this threefold form including fidelity to YHWH with all of one's $m^{e'}\bar{o}d$ in only one other verse in the Scriptures, this Josiah eulogy of 2 Kings 23:25.[16]

The judgment command of Deut. 17:8-12 requires that one "enquire" ($dr\check{s}$) via a priest or judge, at the place which YHWH chooses, what course to take in a difficult judgment. The only king who is ever portrayed as having thus enquired ($dr\check{s}$) of YHWH via a priest at the chosen place on any matter is Josiah, who enquires via the priest Hilkiah concerning the book which Hilkiah has found, 2 Kings 22:13,18. The passage in Deuteronomy, interestingly, is immediately followed by the Deuteronomic law of the king, vv. 13-20. The $dr\check{s}$ command warns the enquiring party, "Do not turn from the thing which they will tell you, to the right or left," (v. 11). The law of the king, requiring that the king write a copy of the Torah and read regularly, likewise explains, ". . . so that he will not turn from the commandment to the right or left," (v. 20; cf. also Deut. 5:29; 28:14). This caution in the form "Do not turn to the right or left" is attached to obedience to the book of the Torah of Moses in two passages in the book of Joshua as well (1:7; 23:6). It occurs nowhere else in Scripture except in the Deuteronomist's evaluation of Josiah, reporting that Josiah did what was right in the eyes of YHWH, went in the path of David, "and he did not turn to the right or left," (2 Kings 22:2).

Josiah's zeal in regard to the book ($s\bar{e}per$) of the Torah is itself another link between Deuteronomy and the Josiah pericope. Indeed, the $s\bar{e}per$ of Moses is mentioned in only three passages in the Deuteronomistic history outside of Deuteronomy and the story of Josiah: Josh. 1:8; 8:31,34; 23:6. Two of these passages are already familiar to us as those relating to obedience without "turning to the right or left," (cf. above).

The Deuteronomist's intended linkage of Moses and Josiah is further manifest in several more parallels of action and phraseology. Moses commands that the Torah be read every seventh year "in the ears" of all the people, tqr' $'t$ $htwrh$ $hz't$ ngd kl $y\acute{s}r'l$ $b'znyhm$ (Deut. 31:11). Josiah gathers all the people and reads the words of the book in their ears, $wyqr'$ $b'znyhm$ (2 Kings 23:2). The idiom occurs only once elsewhere in the history.[17] Moses burns and smashes the

---

[16] I am grateful to Baruch Halpern for sharing this observation with me.

[17] Judg. 7:3; the verb qr' is used here in its sense of *to call* rather than *to read* in the other passages.

golden calf "thin as dust," *daq l^{ec}āpār*, and casts the dust on the wadi, (*nāḥāl*), (Deut. 9:21). At the site of Jeroboam's golden calf of Bethel, Josiah smashes the *bāmāh* and burns it, "and he made it thin as dust (*hedaq l^{ec}āpār*)," (2 Kings 23:15). The dependence of the episode of Aaron's golden calf in JE and Deuteronomic tradition upon the matter of Jeroboam's golden calves at Dan and Bethel has long been noted in scholarly discussion. This equation of the fate of Aaron's calf and that of the calf (or *bāmāh*) of Bethel especially underlines the association of the two in the Deuteronomist's perspective. The particular phraseology occurs twice more in the description of Josiah's zealous actions. Josiah burns the statue of Asherah which Manasseh had set in the Temple, at the wadi (*nāḥāl*) Kidron, "and he made it thin as dust (*wayyādeq l^cāpār*)," (23:6). The phrase *daq l^eāpār* occurs nowhere but in the passages noted here. Josiah also smashes the altars which his ancestors had made and casts their dust into the wadi (v. 12).

This treatment which Josiah accords the altar and statue of Asherah has other direct parallels in the Torah of Moses. The Mosaic law of Deuteronomy 12 specifically commands, "you shall smash (*ntṣ*) their altars ... and burn (*śrp*) their Asherim with fire ..." (Deut. 12:3). Josiah, as remarked above, smashes (*ntṣ*) the altars and burns (*śrp*) the Asherah.[18]

The prohibition of making any graven image (*pesel*) occurs repeatedly in Deuteronomy, both in the Decalogue (Deut. 5:8) and elsewhere (4:16,23,25; 27:15), including an order that a *pesel* of a foreign god be burnt (7:25). The term rarely occurs thereafter -- outside of the book of Judges, the only reference to a *pesel* is among the Samaritans--until Manasseh sets the *pesel* of Asherah in the Temple (2 Kings 21:7). Josiah removes this image and burns it.

The list of associations between Moses' book and the Josiah narrative must certainly include the matter of *sēper hattōrāh* itself. As remarked above, the *sēper* as such is only mentioned in this particular series of passages. The connection, however, is more than terminological. In Deuteronomy, Moses summons the Levites who bear the ark and he instructs them: "Take this book of the Torah (*sēper hattōrāh*) and place it at the side of the ark of the covenant

---

[18] One should observe that the treatment of Hezekiah's similar measures (2 Kings 18) does not portray them in the language of Deuteronomy.

of YHWH your God, and it will be there as a witness against you," (31:26). The book then ceases to be an issue in the history until Hilkiah says, "I have found *sēper hattōrāh* in the house of YHWH," (2 Kings 22:8).[19] Whatever the actual historical circumstances, there can be no doubt of the intent of the Deuteronomistic tradent in the portrayal of history. The first edition of the Deuteronomistic history was the story of the nation and its leaders from Moses to Josiah. The many associations of these two figures clearly constitute an inclusio to the story. The internal association of Josiah and David, the prediction of Josiah's zeal set at the inauguration of Jeroboam's cult, the ratings of each king of Israel and Judah, and the peroration on the fall of the Northern kingdom as proof that offense against the covenant of YHWH would certainly bring disaster — all of these elements united the events of centuries within the inclusio so as to recount history as an ongoing story, meaningful, the issue at all times being ultimately the relationship of YHWH and the people of Israel. This first edition of the Deuteronomistic history (Dtr[1]) properly climaxed in its conclusion, the reform of the Davidid Josiah according to the instruction of Moses. The disasters which struck the nation and the sons and grandson of Josiah were so overwhelming as to demand addition to the history in an Exilic edition (Dtr[2]). The style of the first edition was retained (i.e., imitated) in the supplementary passages. The identification of these Exilic passages is my next task.

2 Kings 21:8-15. Cross has pointed to thematic grounds for regarding this passage, which predicts destruction and exile in the midst of the Manasseh pericope, as the work of the Exilic editor: the unspecific reference to unnamed prophets' oracles against Manasseh and the nation, the lack of any prior prophecies concerning Manasseh's sin and its consequences, the conflict with the attitude of the Dtr[1] edition toward the eternal Davidic promise, and the question of "Why Manasseh?" In addition to these factors, one may discern a syntactic irregularity in the text which points to the precise juncture at which Dtr[2] intervened. The first seven verses of the chapter describe the crimes of Manasseh in terms which relate to the activities of Josiah, i.e., the writer names the wrongs which Josiah set right. Manasseh rebuilds the *bāmôt*, Josiah smashes them. Manasseh sets up the Asherah, Josiah burns it. Manasseh sets altars "to all the host of heaven" in the Temple precincts,

---

[19] Cf. 1 Kings 8:21.

Josiah smashes them. The record of the offenses of Manasseh is thus patently Dtr[1], a fact which is further confirmed by the reference to the Temple as "the house where YHWH would set his name forever," (v. 7), this phrase being the formula of the Deuteronomistic Name theology, which otherwise occurs only in the Dtr[1] passages.[20] The theme of the text subtly shifts immediately following this verse, the shift occurring amidst some syntactic awkwardness, thus:

> (v.7) He set the image of Asherah which he had made in the house of which YHWH had said to David and to Solomon his son, "In this house and in Jerusalem which I have chosen from all the tribes of Israel I shall set my name forever (v. 8) and I shall not cause the foot of Israel to wander from the land which I gave to their fathers only if they will take care to do according to all that I have commanded them and to all the Torah which my servant Moses commanded them."

The matter of concern in v. 7 is the *house*, and the quotation of YHWH which begins in the middle of that verse indeed does focus on the house. The second half of the quotation (v. 8), however, has nothing to do with the house, even though the quotation is specifically introduced in v. 7 as being the words of YHWH with regard to the house ("...in the *house of which YHWH had said...*"). This second half of the quotation rather limits the *forever* of the formula with an "only if," the *forever* being precisely what is important to Dtr[1].

From this juncture through v. 15, the perspective changes. The center of attention becomes the people instead of the king. The historian is only interested in Manasseh as a *maḥăṭiʾ* (*hiphil* factitive), i.e., as one who causes the others to transgress. The unnamed prophets predict the utter destruction of the nation like the destruction of the Northern kingdom. The text then returns in v. 16 to the personal crimes of Manasseh (= Dtr[1]). The Exilic tradent's revision was brilliant with regard to structure. Taking advantage of the portrayal in his received text of the crimes of

---

[20] Cf. Samuel Dean McBride, "The Deuteronomic Name Theology" (Harvard dissertation, 1969). The Name theology is associated with the eternal survival of the House (see 1 Kings 9:3; 11:36); the Exilic Deuteronomist could hardly have developed such a theme.

Manasseh and of Josiah's horror at the pending consequences, the tradent of Dtr^2 expanded the implications of the crimes, emphasized the role of the people, and rendered the eternal Name theology conditional, all without apparently deleting a word of the received edition. The Dtr^2 tradent also began the updating epilogue of the Exilic edition (2 Kings 23:26-25:26) by stating—immediately following the Dtr^1 notice that there arose none like Josiah—that Josiah's short-lived reform did not suffice to offset the crimes of Manasseh. Judah would suffer a fate like that of the Northern kingdom, and YHWH would reject the house of which he had said, "My name will be there." One should note that in this Dtr^2 imitation of the Name theology formula the word *forever* is no longer used.

1 Kings 9:6-9. An extremely similar editorial process is apparent in an expansion of the Dtr^1 portrayal of YHWH's second appearance to Solomon. The Name theology is again present as an eternal promise followed by no conditions (9:3). The following two verses promise that the throne of David will be securely attached to the Davidids forever, but only on condition that they observe the laws of YHWH. The author of this Dtr^1 passage seems to attach a level of conditionality which is directly opposed to the eternal promise which was discussed above,[21] epitomized in 2 Sam. 7:11b-16. Two other passages likewise attach conditions of observance of the law to the promise of the Davidic family's eternal hold on the throne, 1 Kings 2:4 and 8:25. But the common element of all these three passages is the formula *l' ykrt lk 'yš m'l ks' yśr'l*, "there will not be cut off from you a man upon the throne of Israel." It is the throne of *Israel* which is conditional. The references to the eternal dynastic promise, on the other hand, refer to the "throne" or to the "kingdom," but never say "throne of Israel" or "kingdom of Israel" (so 2 Sam. 7:11b-16; 1 Kings 2:45). The passages cited above (pp. 3-4.) concerning the fief which the Davidids retain despite the offenses of Solomon, Abijah, and Jehoram, on the other hand, clearly identify that fief as only Jerusalem/Judah, i.e., the original holding of the Davidic family. This critical distinction between the thrones of Israel and Judah is not a more subtle one than the historian intended. The Deuteronomistic history, on the contrary, maintains the distinction both before and after the division of Jeroboam.[22] One must conclude that the three occurrences of the

---

[21] See above, pp. 3-4.

[22] Cf. 2 Sam. 3:10; 5:5; 1 Kings 1:35; 11:38; 12:19ff.

conditional promise of the throne of Israel—all of which are
addressed to Solomon—are part and parcel of the first edition of the
history and are intended to demonstrate that Solomon had been
duly warned of the consequences of his apostasy.

Following this conditional offer to Solomon in vv. 4f. a
strange shift in the address occurs. Suddenly YHWH is addressing
a plural audience which in context can only be the entire people.[23]
This passage threatens that if the people commit apostasy they will
be cast out of their land and the Temple will be destroyed. The
impossible grammatical transfer and the reference to destruction of
the Temple point to the Exilic hand. Once again the Name theology with its assurance of the eternal survival of the Temple has
been followed with a blatant discarding of that eternal commitment.

What makes this entire combined pericope particularly complex is that the Exilic Deuteronomist refers to the nation as *Israel.*
Since this passage speaks of the destruction of the Temple as well,
it must be referring to the fall of Judah, or to the ultimate demise
of both kingdoms, but definitely does not refer to the Northern
kingdom, as does the passage (discussed above) which precedes it.
The complex mixture of two referents of the name Israel actually
supports the delineation observed here between Dtr[1] (vv. 2-5) and
Dtr[2] (vv. 6-9), because the Dtr[2] reference to the destruction of
Israel with the Temple in it owes to the particular problem of the
Exilic tradent's task. The tradent wishes to insert a prediction of
the final fall of Judah, but the insertion is being made into a point
in the history prior to the division of the kingdoms. Reference to
Judah would be an impossible anachronism. Hence our text.

Deut. 31:16-22; 28-30. The Exilic tradent further inserted
predictions and warnings into the text of Moses' book of the Torah,
including YHWH's last words to Moses prior to summoning him to
his death in Deuteronomy 31. This chapter is one of the most
difficult in the Pentateuch for identification, for three layers are
present. A number of scholars have recognized that the chapter

---

[23] The well-known singular/plural problem in source identification in the book of
Deuteronomy is not an issue here. There it is the nation which is addressed in
singular or plural. Here the case is a change to plural in the midst of an address to
Solomon. The problem in Deuteronomy is discussed by G. Minette de Tillesse,
"Sections 'tu' et sections 'vous' dans le Deuteronome," *VT* 12 (1962), pp. 29-87.
The position of de Tillesse is summarized in E. W. Nicholson, *Deuteronomy and
Tradition,* pp. 27-31.

14

divides neatly into thematic units[24] thus:

vv. 1-8	Moses encourages Joshua and the people
9-13	Moses charges that the Torah be read publicly every seven years
14f., 23	YHWH charges Joshua
16-22	Introduction of the Song of Moses
24-27	Moses charges that the book of the Torah be placed beside the ark
28-30	Introduction of the Song of Moses (continued)

The first two units, vv. 1-13, are Josianic. The instruction that the Torah be "read in the ears" of the people has been discussed above[25] in thematic and phraseological association with the Josiah pericope. Vv. 14f. are anomalous amidst Deuteronomic materials. These verses contain the only mention of the Tent of Meeting (*'ōhel môʿēd*) in Deuteronomy, and they have been properly identified as JE.[26] The instruction that Moses bring Joshua to the Tent to be charged is carried out in v. 23, which is from the same hand. The intervening verses, 16-22, however, break the context and are patently in the Deuteronomistic style. This passage introduces the Song of Moses (Deuteronomy 32) and is modeled upon the song at certain points. The expression "I shall hide my face from them" (31:17f.), for example, derives directly from the striking words of the old song[27] "I shall hide my face from them/I shall

---

[24] Cf. G.E. Wright, *Deuteronomy, The Interpreter's Bible* II, p. 515; Nicholson, *Deuteronomy and Tradition,* p. 19; S. R. Driver, *Introduction to the Literature of the Old Testament,*, pp. 71f., (hereafter cited as *ILOT*).

[25] P. 8.

[26] Cf. Driver, *ILOT*, p. 31; Weinfeld, *DDS*, p. 191n.

[27] On the date of the Song of Moses, long preceding Dtr[1] and Dtr[2], see G.E. Wright, "The Lawsuit of God: A Form-Critical Study of Deuteronomy 32," in *Israel's Prophetic Heritage*, B. Anderson and W. Harrelson, eds., pp. 26-67; W.F. Albright, "Some Remarks on the Song of Moses in Deuteronomy XXXII," *VT* 9

see what their end will be" (32:20). The preceding line of the song states, "and YHWH saw and spurned," an expression which likewise appears in the introduction, thus: ". . . and they caused me to spurn (or spurned me) . . ." (31:20). In the introduction, YHWH declares that he will one day leave his people and hide his face from them.[28] This is not presented as a threat but as a revelation of an actual future event. It is the work of an Exilic hand.

Following these JE and Exilic units, the text returns to the matter of Moses' instructions regarding *sēper hattōrāh,* vv. 24-27. The writer explains in v. 24 that what follows is the instruction which Moses had made at the time of his completion of the book. Some scholars have regarded this passage as a doublet of vv. 9-13, but it is certainly not. Both the charge to read the Torah publicly and the charge to set the book beside the ark as a witness were integral to the Deuteronomistic (Dtr[1]) interest, and each has a reflex in the Josiah narrative, as discussed above. The notice of Moses' completion of the book may be simply the epanalepsis of Dtr[1] flowing from the Josianic writer's extended explanation of the public readings (vv. 12b,13) or may be the epanalepsis of Dtr[2] upon the conclusion of the Exilic writer's insertion into his received text.

V. 28 begins with Moses' instruction to the Levites to summon all the elders of the tribes. But, in the Dtr[1] account, all the elders of Israel are already standing in front of Moses. The theme of vv. 28f. and its language further confirm that this is once again the hand of the Dtr[2] tradent. The subject is once again the song which YHWH has instructed Moses to teach the people. Moses now fulfills this instruction and presents the song as a witness against Israel. Again the tradent's choice of wording is based on the words of the song. Moses announces that he will call heaven and earth to witness (v. 28). This of course refers to the opening bicolon of the song, which does just that:

(1959), pp. 339-346: Cross, *CMHE,* p. 264n. The influence of this song upon Exilic writing in Deuteronomy has been noted by Jon Levenson, "Who Inserted the Book of the Torah?" *HTR* 68 (1975), p. 217. Actually the influence of the song is apparent in Dtr[1] and Jeremiah as well, and so it must not be used for source identification but rather only for analysis of the editorial process and interests of the Deuteronomistic literature. Cf. references in Weinfeld's collection of Deuteronomistic phraseology (above, n. 11).

[28] On the phrase "I shall hide my face," see R.E. Friedman, "The Biblical Expression *mastîr pānîm,*" *HAR* 1 (1977), pp. 139-147.

16

Give ear O heaven and I shall speak
And hear O earth the words of my mouth

(32:1)

The causative *šḥt* (to corrupt) of 31:29 matches the *piel* form of that verb in the song, 32:5. The reference to the end of days (*'aḥărît hayyāmîm*) and the angering of YHWH (31:29) probably relate to terms in the song as well; cf. 32:16,19,20.

S. R. Driver observed this break between Deut. 31:24-27 and 28-30 and also ascribed them to separate authors [29] but failed to identify the latter as more than an unknown redactor. Others[30] regarded the two passages as a unity, thus forcing themselves to postulate emendations in the text to resolve difficulties. The similarity of the thus-united passage to vv. 16-22 led many commentators to replace the word *Torah* in v. 24 with the word *song*. Von Rad expressed confidence that the case was the reverse; the word *song* in vv. 16-22 was to be replaced with *Torah*.[31] Such emendations are utterly unnecessary in the light of the evidence for the work of two editors here.

Following the introduction of the Song of Moses, the Exilic tradent inserted the text of the song itself (Deut. 32:1-43) and added a single-verse resumption of the narrative (cf. 31:30; 32:44). This is followed by a beautifully worded conclusion (Dtr[1]) in which Moses emphasizes for a third time that the events of this day constitute a witness against the people with regard to their future actions (Deut. 32:45-47).

In addition to attaching the introduction, conclusion, and text of the Song of Moses to the end of the Josianic tradent's edition of Deuteronomy, the Exilic tradent inserted a number of passages into the body of the text, thus:

Deut. 4:25-31. It has been argued that Deut. 4:1-40 is a unity and Exilic, most recently by Norbert Lohfink and Jon Levenson.[32]

---

[29] See above, n. 24.

[30] Nicholson, see above, n. 24.

[31] Von Rad, *Deuteronomy, A Commentary*, p. 190.

[32] Norbert Lohfink, "Auslegung deuteronomischer Texte, IV," *Bibel und Leben* 5 (1964), pp. 250-253; Levenson, "Who Inserted the Book of the Torah?" pp. 203-233.

Levenson's defense of Lohfink's position is discussed below.[33] Lohfink recognizes a thematic division of the chapter into units of vv. 1-24, 25-31, and 32-40, and he further notes the particular Exile/restoration orientation of the second unit. He nonetheless associates this second unit with the one which precedes it on the grounds that the second unit naturally continues the discussion of the prohibition of making a *pesel* (v. 25), which is the final concern of the first unit (v. 23). In response to Lohfink, one must simply recognize the possibility that the Exilic Deuteronomist was clever-enough an editor to think of associating his insertions with his received text. As seen in the texts which we have examined thus far, this Exilic tradent was expert at just this. In the present text, nothing of vv. 1-24 demands an Exilic date. On the contrary, the prohibition of the *pesel*, as noted above, [34] finds dramatization in the Manasseh/Josiah pericopes. Vv. 25-31, moreover, generates a significant thematic interference with the units which precede and follow it. These units emphasize the angry side of the character of YHWH, characterizing him as *'ēl qannā'* (jealous God; v. 24) and particularly emphasizing the image of his consuming fire repeatedly (vv. 11,12,15,24,33,36). But in the midst of this fiery warning comes a promise that even in the event of exile the people may seek YHWH and find him, he will not destroy them, he will not forget his covenant with them, because he is *'ēl raḥûm* (merciful God; v. 31)! The text then reverts to fiery warning. It is this very theme of hope and restoration which has identified vv. 25-31 as Exilic in years of scholarly discussion,[35] and it is in this softening of the threat of the received text that we once again see the editorial work of Dtr^2 remodeling the Josianic interests of Dtr^1 so as to fit Exilic interests, without apparently deleting a word.

In addition to these thematic grounds, certain matters of phraseology further indicate the Exilic character of vv.25-31. Notably, the words "I call heaven and earth to witness against you" (v. 26) are a recurrence of the expression cited above as deriving from the Song of Moses. Also recurring are the reference to the end of days and the notion that troubles will "find" the people in the

---

[33] Levenson's treatment can only be considered following the discussion of Deuteronomy 29 and 30, on which his argument depends, below.

[34] See above, pp. 10f.

[35] Alfred Bertholet regarded vv. 25-31 as an Exilic addition and recognized that vv. 32ff. continue from vv. 1-24; *Deuteronomium* (1899), pp. 13-15.

absence of the protection of YHWH (v. 30), both of which occur in the Exilic portions of Deuteronomy 31.

Another indicator that this passage was addressed to an Exilic audience is its extreme similarity to the letter which Jeremiah sends to the exiles in Babylon shortly before the fall of Jerusalem. Moses declares:

> *wbqštm mšm 't yhwh 'lhyk wmṣ't*
> *ky tdršnw bkl lbbk wbkl npšk*

And you will seek YHWH your God from there
and you will find him, when you seek him
out with all your heart and all your soul.

Deut. 4:29

Jeremiah writes:

> *wbqštm 'ty wmṣ'tm*
> *ky tdršny bkl lbbkm*

And you will seek me and you will find me, when you
seek me out with all your heart.

Jer. 29:13

On literary, thematic, phraseological, and comparative grounds, therefore, Deut. 4:25-31 must be regarded as Exilic.

Deut. 29:21-27. Lohfink and Levenson have noted the Exilic character of this passage.[36] The syntactic indicator of the insertion is the change-over of subject. From a threat concerning an individual man or woman who might sin (29:17,19) and the consequences for that individual (*bā'iš hahū'*), the text suddenly turns in v. 21 to speaking as if the subject had been the entire nation. The nation is pictured as having been cast out of its land. As in the Dtr[2] insertion into the Jerusalem revelation of Solomon discussed above, the author here portrays someone as asking, "Why has YHWH done thus to this land?" (Deut. 29:23 = 1 Kings 9:8), to which the response is:

---

[36] Lohfink, "Auslegung deuteronomischer Texte," pp. 44f.; Levenson, "Who Inserted the Book of the Torah?" p. 208.

And they will say, "Because they left the
covenant of YHWH the God of their fathers
which he made with them when he brought
them out of the land of Egypt, and they
went and served other gods and bowed to them ..."

Deut. 29:24,25a

And they will say, "Because they left YHWH their
God who brought them out of the land of Egypt, and
they took hold of other gods and bowed to them
and served them ... "

1 Kings 9:9a

The hand of an Exilic writer, the tradent of Dtr[2], seems to be at work here.

Deut. 30:1-10. G. E. Wright has pointed out that, following the passage just discussed, the last verse of Deuteronomy 29 connects properly to vv. 11-14 of Deuteronomy 30.[37] Thus united, the passage 29:29; 30:11-14 compares the "hidden things," which belong to YHWH, to the commandment of YHWH, which is "close to you, in your mouth and in your heart, to do it." The text which intersects the unity of this passage, Deut. 30:1-10, is clearly from the same writer as the other Exilic additions identified thus far. Some affinities of this pericope to the Exilic portion of Deuteronomy 4 are present, leading Wolff and Levenson to speak in terms of a late bracketing of the original Deuteronomic corpus.[38] Phraseologically, the expression of YHWH's scattering (*hēpîṣ*) the nations occurs in both of these pericopes. This *hiphil* expression never occurs in Dtr[1] or in the older portions of Deuteronomy; the notion is very common, however, in other Exilic writings, particularly Jeremiah and Ezekiel. Thematically as well, the words of Deut. 30:1-10 look strikingly Exilic, addressing an exiled community, declaring that restoration is possible, referring to the mercy of YHWH, pointing to the return to YHWH which is necessary in order to bring about this reconciliation.

---

[37] Wright, *Deuteronomy*, p. 507.

[38] Wolff, "Kerygma," pp. 182f.

20

Deut. 30:15-20. Following the passage which was noted above to be intersected by the Exilic 30:1-10, a second Exilic passage has been added in 30:15-20. Many scholars, most recently Levenson,[39] have regarded 30:1-20 as a unity, apparently without taking notice of the continuity of 29:29 to 30:11-14. Levenson acknowledges that the transition from 30:1-10 to 30:11ff. "is not without problems," and he takes 29:28 to be a "pious gloss." The fact is that there is good evidence for identifying 1-10 and 15-20 with other Exilic passages, and little for 11-14. This fact is especially underlined by Lohfink's having had to look for such evidence in comparing the notion of the nearness of the commandment in 11:14 with the notion of the nearness of God in Exilic (sic!) Deuteronomy 4:7.[40] The comparison is weak; and in any event the view of this portion of Deuteronomy 4 as Exilic has been questioned above.

The wording of 30:15-20 is certainly consistent with other Exilic passages. The declaration "I call heaven and earth to witness against you" recurs (v. 19), which certainly derives from the Exilic tradent's presentation of the Song of Moses and occurs in Deut. 4:26 as well. Also recalling 4:26 is the infinitival emphatic *'ābōd tō'bēdûn* of 30:18. The theme of the passage is the duration of the nation on the land and the threat of apostasy to that duration. It is Exilic.

As remarked above, Jon Levenson has argued in defense of Lohfink's view of Deut. 4:1-40 as a unity. Discussion of Levenson's argument was necessarily withheld until this point because it is dependent upon a recognition of the Exilic character of Deut. 29:21-27; 30, a fact which has now been discussed and agreed to here (with the exception of 30:11-14). Levenson offers a list of linguistic and stylistic correspondences between Deut. 29:21-27; 30 and portions of Deuteronomy 4, including the sections preceding and following the one section which is regarded here as Exilic (4:25-31).[41] Levenson notes that 4:19 and 29:25 are the only examples in Scripture of the verb *ḥlq* in context of distributing gods to the nations; 4:19 and 30:17 are the only instances of the conjunction of the roots *ndḥ* and *ḥwh*; 4:32 and 30:4 share the expression

---

[39] Levenson, "Who Inserted the Book of the Torah?" pp. 208f.

[40] Lohfink, "Auslegung deuteronomischer Texte," p. 42n.

[41] Levenson, "Who Inserted the Book of the Torah?" pp. 212-215.

(known outside Dtr) "end of the heavens;" 4:39 and 30:1 share *whv̌sbt 'l lbbk* which occurs elsewhere only in Exilic passages (including 1 Kings 8:47); 4:16 and 31:29 are "the only explicit attestations of *v̌sht* to indicate material idolatry in the future." The problem in dealing with such parallels of terms or styles is that the Deuteronomistic literature seems to be the product of a "school" in the sense that there is definitely conscious imitation of style and repetition or reinforcement of themes. We have already seen examples of the skill with which the Dtr^2 tradent wrote and edited within the framework of a received text. That stylistic unity accounts for the widespread acceptance of the Noth hypothesis of a single Deuteronomist even among those, such as von Rad and Wolff, who recognized thematic difficulties therein. Indeed, the similarity of the Deuteronomistic works over a considerable span of time is extraordinary. Moshe Weinfeld's collection of Deuteronomic (*sic!*) phraseology is impressive—and not exhaustive.[42] The difficulty in separating sources along phraseological grounds is portrayed by Levenson's pointing to 1 Kings 8:47 as an Exilic parallel to his fourth pairing. The passage 8:46-53 has often been regarded as Exilic, but this is hardly certain. In the passage, Solomon asks that if ever the people sin and therefore suffer defeat and are taken captive, YHWH listen to their prayer which they direct toward the land, the city (Jerusalem), and the *Temple*. The full context of the chapter is consistently in reference to the Temple as channel to YHWH. How could an Exilic author write such a thing? One might suggest that the Temple had to be mentioned to avoid anachronism or inconsistency with context. But surely it would have been better to write nothing at all than to inform exiles that their channel to salvation is the building which no longer exists. The idiom which Levenson notes here and in Deuteronomy is thus common to Dtr^1 and Dtr^2.

The point of these remarks is not to suggest that phraseological and stylistic evidence may not be useful. On the contrary, they are used regularly in the present work. But they are helpful only when studied in the presence of literary and thematic grounds for division or in the types of mutually-supporting colloquies which are particularly compelling. Levenson relies upon Lohfink's arguments for thematic grounds, but these, as argued here, are doubtful. On literary grounds Levenson sees an interference at 4:1 into a text

[42] See above, n. 11.

which originally flowed from the first three chapters of the book directly into 31:1. But it is equally likely that the reason why these sections appear to flow so well is that the author of Deut. 1-3 and 31:1ff. intentionally set the command to charge Joshua in the first section and set the ceremonial charge in the second so as to enclose the material between them (the old core of Deuteronomy plus his own non-historical material) in the midst of a historical framework. This would constitute an inclusio of Deuteronomy at the hand of the editor who likewise constructed the Moses/Josiah inclusio discussed above. As for the juncture of chapters 3 and 4, G. E. Wright has regarded 4:1ff. not as a break but as the climax of the address of Moses.[43] The parallels which Levenson brings in support of Lohfink are by no means weak, and the possibility that they point to a larger Exilic insertion than 4:25-31 must be considered, but Lohfink's own presentation does not establish this. The evidence to the contrary which is presented above suggests, rather, that the Exilic tradent's work was a relatively limited one, adding only passages which expressed the crucial interests of the Exilic situation.

Deut. 28:36f. These two verses break context with the portions of the Deuteronomic curse list which surround them. In the midst of a group of curses which relate to miseries of the body and of the land comes this threat of exile for the people and their king among many nations. The curses which follow, however, do not relate to exile at all, but rather presume the presence of the people in the land. The intrusion of these verses into the structure of the pericope, together with the exilic theme of the intruding verses, suggests secondary Exilic addition.

Deut. 28:63-68. At this juncture in the curse list there appears an exception to the specific curses which have filled the chapter. V. 63 is rather a terrifying dramatization of the attitude of YHWH toward the people if they will break his covenant.

> And it will be that, as YHWH rejoiced over you to do
> you good and to multiply you, so will YHWH rejoice
> over you to destroy you and annihilate you.

What follows is a threat of eviction from the land and scattering of the people among the nations. This is the third encounter with the phrase "scatter (*hēpîṣ*) among the nations," and this exhausts their

---

[43] Wright, *Deuteronomy*, p. 350.

appearances in Dtr. As for the rejoicing of YHWH, first to do good and then to do harm, the hope which is offered in the Exilic passage Deut. 30:1-10 includes the turnaround: "YHWH will turn back to rejoice over you for good as he rejoiced over your fathers." This particular parallel must be regarded cautiously, for the 30:1-10 passage also turns around some of the older curses of Deuteronomy 28. Still, this particular expression occurs only in these two places and in the prison speech of Jeremiah, which is dated in the text to within a year on the fall of Jerusalem (Jer. 32:41). While a threat of exile does not necessarily mark a passage as Exilic—it was a common entry in seventh-century treaty curse lists[44] —the combination of the exile intimidation, the phraseological associations and the stylistic juncture at v. 63 indicates the presence of Dtr². The last curse of the list is the ultimate threat in the story of the people of Israel, namely that YHWH will cause them to return to Egypt. This extraordinary statement of a return to the *status quo* which existed prior to Israel's meeting with YHWH and formation as an independent people concludes with the horror: "and you will sell yourselves there to your enemies as slaves, ad no one will buy," (v. 68). The implications of this curse, which has never been properly weighed and reckoned with, will be discussed at length below.

Deut. 8:19f. The text of Deut. 8:1-18 forewarns the people that when prosperity prevails in their new land they are not to attribute their well-being to their own powers. They must remember the power of YHWH which brought them out of Egypt and maintained them in the wilderness; this is the power which provides plenty for the land. Deuteronomy 9 similarly forewarns the people not to attribute the coming conquest of the land to their own merit. The short passage which intervenes between these related pericopes is a two-verse threat concerning apostasy. The consequence is destruction. The language is familiar. The expression *'ābōd tō'bēdûn* recurs, and this exhausts its appearances. The passage thus appears to be Exilic.

A few passages remain which are less certain of identification than those discussed thus far but which are sufficiently suspicious as to summon scrutiny.

Josh. 23:15f. Following Joshua's announcement that everything which YHWH has promised has come true, this passage brings the tidings back down with the reminder that just as YHWH

---

[44] See Delbert Hillers, *Treaty-Curses and the Old Testament Prophets*, pp. 33f.

has brought the promised good he can bring the promised destruction of the people off the land if they break covenant. The language includes some of the most common phrases of Dtr, rendering dating on these grounds hazardous. The point of the text nonetheless appears Exilic.

1 Kings 6:11-13. The epanalepsis of "And Solomon built the house and completed it" (vv. 9 and 14) marks this passage concerning the Davidic promise as an insertion. The question is whether it is an insertion of the Josianic tradent (Dtr[1]) into his source or the insertion of the Exilic tradent (Dtr[2]) into the received Dtr[1] edition. The conditional portrayal of the Davidic promise may suggest that this is another Dtr[1] explanation of the loss of the Northern kingdom because of the offenses of Solomon. The difference between this passage and the other such explanatory passages (discussed above, pp. 14-16), however, is that the apodosis of each of the other propositions relates to the disposition of the throne. The apodosis of this passage refers instead to YHWH's continuing presence in Israel. He will not *leave* his people. The passage may belong to Dtr[2].[45]

2 Kings 17:19. In the midst of the peroration on the fall of the Northern kingdom, this verse adds, seemingly parenthetically, "Judah also did not observe the commandments of YHWH their God, and they went by the standards of Israel which they did." It is perhaps conceivable that this is Dtr[1] developing the theme of wrongdoing in Judah as background of the reforms of Hezekiah and Josiah. Linguistic evidence does not appear, unfortunately, and so the awkwardness of the verse in context is the chief reason for suspecting an Exilic addition.

2 Kings 17:35-40a. Definite thematic and stylistic evidence for the Exilic date of this passage is not readily apparent, but the presence of epanalepsis and syntactic chaos argues for insertion into a Dtr[1] narrative. According to that narrative, the Samaritans "act according to their former customs" and do not follow the laws "which YHWH commanded the children of Jacob whose name he made Israel," (v. 34). The verses which follow leave off the Samaritans and relate the words of YHWH's covenant with the people, concluding in v. 40a: "but they did not listen. . ." The second half of v. 40 now comes and identifies the subject of "but *they* did

---

[45] The similarity of the passage to Priestly language further demands caution in dating.

not listen" as not the people of Israel, but the Samaritans! Thus: "but they did not listen, but rather they act according to their former custom." 17:35-40a must be an insertion. The material which it intersects is stylisticly Deuteronomistic, as is the insertion. Both Dtr[1] and Dtr[2] are apparently present.[45a]

2 Kings 22:16-20. The complexity of the double prophecy of the prophetess Huldah, half of which is directed to the "man who sent you to me," half to the king of Judah, is perplexing. There is no outright prediction of Exile. Are the prophecies of approaching calamity the work of Dtr[1], portraying the terrifying message which prompts Josiah to action, or are they the work of Dtr[2], predicting the destruction? Is the promise that Josiah will die in peace the writing of Dtr[1], unaware that Josiah is to die from the wound of an Egyptian arrow, or is it the writing of Dtr[2], regarding Josiah's death as taking place during the peaceful moments prior to the Babylonian disaster? The difficulty is increased by the similarity of Huldah's wording to the wording of Jeremiah's description of the disaster in retrospect, Jer. 44:3-6 (cf. 42:18). Cross regards the content of the prophecy of Huldah as Exilic insertion, though based on some old nucleus. In short, both the Josianic and Exilic hands may be present here in an editorial combination which is too complex to unravel.

The work of the Exilic Deuteronomist, in sum, is observable in these passages:

Deut. 4:24-31
8:19f.
28:36f.
28:63-68
29:21-27
30:1-10
30:15-20
31:16-22
31:28-30

[45a] J. Gray recognizes both that the passage is an insertion and that it is Deuteronomistic in character, and thus identifies the passage as later than the "first Deuteronomist;" *I and II Kings*, 2nd ed., p. 477. M. Cogan's recent suggestion that the passage refers to the Israelites in Assyrian exile and is itself Josianic exceeds the information given by the inserted text itself, nor does he explain what editorial process is involved in the text and the insertion; "Israel in Exile—the View of a Josianic Historian," *JBL* 97 (1978), pp. 40-44.

                    32:44; plus the song of Moses inserted
        Josh.   (23:15f.)
    1 Kings (6:11-13)
              9:6-9
    2 Kings (17:19)
             (17:35-40a)
             21:8-15
             (22:16-20)
             23:26-25:26(27-30)[46]

II. The editorial work of the Exilic Deuteronomist (Dtr[2])

Once the Exilic passages have been identified, one can observe the interests of each edition of the Deuteronomistic history and judge the impact of the Exilic writer and his age upon the final character of the work. The interest of the first edition (Dtr[1]), on which the Exilic tradent worked, is in the first place the Torah of Moses. The kings and the people are rated according to its criteria. Dtr[1] commences not with Creation or the Patriarchs, but with Moses. The climax of the account lies in the realization of the commands of the book of the Torah at the command of Josiah. Levenson has argued that much of the core of the book of Deuteronomy (5:1-28:68) is at odds with the interests of Dtr[1] and that, therefore, this corpus (Dtn) must have been inserted later, by the tradent who assembled Dtr[2].[47] All that is attributable to Dtr[1], according to Levenson, is the account of Deut. 1-3 and its continuation in 31:1ff. The first of the conflicts of interest between Dtr[1] and Dtn to be considered is the presence of two different views of covenant. The Dtn covenant between YHWH and Israel threatens that the people will perish from the land, owing to the cessation of the land's fertility, in the event of apostasy (Deut. 11:13-17). Levenson, like Matitiahu Tsevat,[48] finds this possibility

---

[46] See below, pp. 57-59.

[47] Levenson, "Who Inserted the Book of the Torah?" pp. 223-231.

[48] Matitiahu Tsevat, "Studies in the Book of Samuel, III," *HUCA* 34 (1963), p. 73.

to be in tension with the Dtr[1] view of the Davidic promise as being eternal. If the people perish, then over whom is the Davidid to reign? One cannot be certain, however, that the difference here is irreconcilable. The Deuteronomy 11 passage wraps the Israelite covenant in the folds of the Patriarchal promise, which in JE, Priestly, and Deuteronomic traditions is much like that of David. It is a promise of land and descendants, possibly forever.[49] The threats may be directed at any given generation, the possibility of revival remaining open to those which follow. This by no means conflicts with the Davidic commitment, which likewise threatens disaster on any given generation, but guarantees the future of the line. One must also consider the reverse prospect, namely that the Davidic promise did not allow for unchecked apostasy either, but rather that here, too, there was a breaking point.[50] Finally, the possibility remains that the passage which Levenson notes is itself another Dtr[2] addition. While evidence was not sufficient to include it among the Dtr[2] passages above, one must yet note that the key statement of the passage is "and you will perish quickly from the good land which YHWH gives to you;" and this expression recurs precisely only in Josh. 23:13,16, which Levenson himself regards as Exilic. Similar expressions occur in Deut. 4:26; 8:19; 30:18, all of which are reckoned above as Exilic. This certainly raises sufficient doubt that this passage was ever part of the Dtn which the Dtr[1] tradent handled to challenge Levenson's argument.

Levenson sees a second conflict between Dtn and Dtr[1] on the matter of the role of the monarchy. Dtn, according to Levenson, is anti-monarchical, regarding not the king but the prophet as the central figure. Josiah as covenant mediator seems to Levenson, and to Noth,[51] to appropriate the prophetic task. The Deuteronomic view of the king, however, is not properly "antimonarchical," but seeks only to place controls on the king and to retain a degree of power

---

[49] The measure, "like the days of the heavens over the earth," (Deut. 11:21) may refer to the duration of the promise or of the people's prospects. The referent is not certain.

[50] See my paper, "Covenant Fidelity and Covenant Stipulation in the Davidic Dynastic Traditions," (unpublished, Harvard Hebrew 200, 1973). I have revised my views concerning this matter considerably since the presentation of this paper, but it still raises doubt as to whether any promissory covenant was unconditional even to the point of outright betrayal of the covenant donor.

[51] Noth, *UGS*, p. 94.

in the hands of priests and prophets (Deut. 17:14-20). This is perfectly consistent with the view of Dtr[1], especially in the matter of Josiah. Josiah accepts the instruction of the book of the Torah to enquire of priest and prophet, i.e., Hilkiah and Huldah, and acts precisely as the executive branch, obeying the Torah legislation as prescribed by Huldah via Hilkiah.

Levenson points to the uncriticized accounts of rural sacrifices in Dtr[1] as a third deviation from the standards of Deuteronomy, which requires centralization at "the place which YHWH will choose," (Deut. 12:13ff.). He points to the sacrifices of Gideon (Judg. 6:11ff.), Samuel (1 Sam. 7:7ff.), Saul (1 Sam. 14:31-35), and Elijah (1 Kings 18:30ff.). The chosen place, however, is in Deuteronomistic reckoning the city in which the ark resides. In the case of Gideon, where was the ark? Perhaps in Bethel (Judges 20), perhaps unapproachable because of the Midianite power (6:2). Gideon's replacing an altar of Baal with one of YHWH as a rally would not necessarily draw criticism even from the author of Dtn. The sacrifices of Samuel and Saul likewise took place at a time when there could not have been a "place." The ark had been stored at Kiryat Yearim for twenty years (1 Sam. 7:2). As for Elijah's sacrifice on Carmel, the prophet was dealing with the kingdom of Israel, but the ark was in Judah. Where else could he go? Further, a story of miraculous fire falling from heaven is hardly a customary sort of sacrifice, and need be consistent with no statutes.

The Deuteronomic prohibition of marriage with the conquered peoples of Canaan is the next interest of Levenson (Deut. 7:3f). He points out that Solomon is not criticized for his intermarriages, but only for the apostasy which results (1 Kings 11:4). The case is in fact the opposite. The injunction in Deuteronomy is one of the few Biblical laws which include a statement of the reason for the demand. Intermarriage is forbidden because the foreign partner will turn the Israelite to apostasy (Deut. 7:4). This is precisely the perspective of 1 Kings 11:1-4. Deut. 7:4 warns that this will enrage YHWH; 1 Kings 11:9 reports that "YHWH was angered at Solomon." The two passages are utterly consistent. Levenson argues that it must be the apostasy, and not the intermarriage, which Dtr[1] criticizes, for there is no criticism of David's marriage to the daughter of the king of Geshur. But the Geshurites, who resided to the East of the Sea of Galilee in Aram, are not among the seven nations which the injunction of Deuteronomy 7 names. The Geshurites, rather, were not expelled by the Israelites, but continued to dwell in the midst of Israel (Josh. 13:13).

Levenson's final conflict between Deuteronomic law and Dtr[1] is based on Albrecht Alt's observation that the country priests' celebrating in their villages rather than Jerusalem during Josiah's Passover (2 Kings 23:9) violates the Deuteronomic rule of centrality of the Passover celebration (Deut. 16:6f.).[52] Alt's reading of 2 Kings 23:9 is the source of the problem. That verse reads thus:

> But the priests of the *bāmôt* did not go up to the altar of YHWH in Jerusalem, but they ate *maṣṣôt* in the midst of their brothers.

This verse has nothing whatever to do with Passover. The Passover pericope of the Josiah narrative begins in v. 21. Alt apparently associated v. 9 with Passover because of the reference to *maṣṣôt* (unleavened cakes). *Maṣṣôt* however, were the required food to be eaten with sacrifices in the Temple (Lev. 6:9f.; cf. Exod. 23:18; Lev. 2:11; 7:11; 8:2; 10:12). The sense of 2 Kings 23:9 is that the country priests, newly moved to Jerusalem, were not permitted to join their "brothers," the Jerusalem priests, in the sacrificial rites of the altar, but of course received their share of the sacrificed meat and the accompanying *maṣṣôt*.[53]

The core of the book of Deuteronomy (Dtn) was not in conflict with the aims of the Josianic Deuteronomist (Dtr[1]). The discussion above of the inclusio of the Josianic edition from Moses to Josiah argues rather that Dtn was in fact crucial to the perspective of Dtr[1].

A reckoning of the interests of Dtr[1] must certainly include the matter of centralization of worship. The sin of Jeroboam thus becomes overwhelming, constituting grounds for categorizing every king of Israel as performing evil. Jeroboam is the *maḥăṭî'* of Israel. The sin of Jeroboam is named in 2 Kings 17 along with the ultimate offense, the worship of other gods, as bringing about the destruction of the nation.[54] The *bāmôt* of Judah, though not portrayed as being as serious an offense as Jeroboam's altars in the North, are

---

[52] Albrecht Alt, "Die Heimat des Deuteronomiums," *Kleine Schrifte zur Geschichte des Volkes Israel*, II, pp. 255-259.

[53] The matter of the unleavened cakes which accompany sacrifices is discussed more fully with regard to Deuteronomistic and Priestly tradition below, Chapter II.

[54] The description of Israel's apostasy, separated from the description of the sin of Jeroboam by the Exilic 17:19, may be Exilic.

nonetheless the fault on the record of every king except Hezekiah and Josiah. Jerusalem and its house, the place toward which one is to direct prayer, the sole place of sanctioned sacrifice, the place where YHWH has caused his name to dwell, are the focus through which the entire history of the monarchies is recounted.

A third interest of the Josianic Deuteronomist is the matter of *'ĕlōhîm 'ăḥērîm*. The exclusive worship of YHWH in the land is an absolute in every book of the work. Even the book of Judges, which is almost entirely a received text, bears the stamp of the Dtr[1] perspective in an introduction which sets a *Leitmotif* upon the old stories which follow (Judg. 2:11-23). The issue is at all times Israel's fidelity to the God with whom they have entered into covenant. Worship of other gods, whether as alternative or as supplement to the service of YHWH, is impossible.

With the Torah as standard for the nation, the centralization of worship, and the prohibition of foreign worship as three foci of the work of Dtr[1], the necessary fourth issue is chastisement. The Josianic tradent—as well as his sources—portrayed the people and its monarchs as almost constantly provoking YHWH beyond the reaches of his well-known compassion. Chastisement may be delayed, as in the survival of the Northern kingdom long past its condemnation, but once due it is not forgotten. The survival of the Southern kingdom may be more secure, owing to the Davidic promises, but some form of chastisement is due in the Dtr[1] portrayal. Though the first edition of the Deuteronomistic history does not forewarn exile, the writer portrays Josiah as acting in terror before the recompense which years of offense have summoned. This leads to another concern of the Josianic tradent: testimony of things to come. Von Rad has observed the frequency of specific prophecy/fulfillment notices in the history.[55] Only one of the notices which von Rad collected is certainly Dtr[2], and, as Cross has noted,[56] it is the only such notice in which no specific prophet or prophecy is identified. Dtr[1] is careful to demonstrate that the word of YHWH does not fail to realize. This is crucial to the climax of the first edition of the work, because the issue is the words of Moses' book. Moses instructs the Levites to set the book beside the ark, ". . . and it will be there as a witness against you." In Dtr[1],

---

[55] N. 14 above.

[56] *CMHE*, p. 286.

written witness has been present during the entire course of the national history.

Against this curtain of witness, threat, offense, and imminent calamity stands the Davidic promise, attached first to the court history of David—which the Deuteronomist inserted into the work—and developed at several later junctures in the history.[57] It is the crucial basis of preservation in the reigns of such kings as Abijah, Jehoram, and Manasseh; and it constitutes grounds for hope of renewal in the reigns of such as Asa, Jehoshaphat, Hezekiah, and Josiah. In its broadest sense, the commitment provides more than the maintenance of the line of David. It means the eternal survival of the City of David and the tribe of Judah. Above all, it guarantees the perpetuation of the Temple as a channel of communication with YHWH, whose presence there is somehow possible as expressed in the Deuteronomistic Name theology.[58]

The interests of Dtr[1] must include the person of Josiah, in whom resides the hope of fulfilling the standards and the hopes which are expressed in the book of the Torah of Moses, and in whose hand lies the restoration of the Kingdom of David as a united community of all Israel with Jerusalem its religious/political center. The Moses/Josiah inclusio is not only a literary device, but a reflection of the Deuteronomist's purpose in writing a directed history rather than annals of historical data.

Finally, an interest of the first edition of the Deuteronomistic history remains which is often overlooked precisely because it is so fundamental to the story and so regularly mentioned, namely Egypt. Beside the fact that Egypt is regularly a political and military issue through the course of the history, the experience of Egyptian bondage and Exodus are ever a temporal and thematic focus of the historian and of his sources. The Exodus from Egypt is the premise of the Decalogue (Deut. 5:6), the only historical datum of the historical prologue.[59] The covenant itself is associated with the

---

[57] Pp. 3-4. above.

[58] McBride, "Deuteronomic Name Theology." "The šēm theologoumenon. . . protected, assured the reality of God's dynamic immanence at the chosen shrine without localizing him there," p. 209.

[59] Klaus Baltzer has particularly stressed the role of the historical prologue as the grounds on which the covenant relations are built in the Hittite covenant models (though absent in the later Assyrian type). Personal communication. See his study of Near Eastern and Biblical covenant, *The Covenant Formulary*, and G. E. Mendenhall, *Law and Covenant in Israel and the Ancient Near East*.

Exodus (1 Kings 8:9,21; cf. Deut. 4:20). The most blatant difference between the Decalogue as it appears in Deuteronomy and its counterpart in the Priestly work is that the Deuteronomic Sabbath command bases the observance of the Sabbath not on the seven-day creation, as in the Priestly work, but on the memory of slavery in Egypt (Deut. 5:15; cf. Exod. 20:11). Numerous other laws are followed by this same formula: "And you will remember that you were a slave in Egypt, therefore I command you to do this thing," (Deut. 16:12; 24:18,22);[60] and in the famous passage which has appropriately become a part of the Jewish Passover *sēder*, Deut. 6:20-25, the entire body of law is predicated upon YHWH's having brought Israel out of Egyptian slavery. Passover is of course the key celebration of the Josianic reform as well (2 Kings 23:21-23). The memory of YHWH's power against Egypt is posited as a source of confidence in future battles (Deut. 1:29f.; 7:18; 20:1). The law of the king forbids the monarch to bring the people back to Egypt "for YHWH has said to you 'you will not ever go back this way again,'" (17:16). The historical creeds of Deut. 26:5-9 and Josh. 24:2-13 which, together with that of Deut. 6:20-25 (mentioned above), were regarded by von Rad as central to understanding Israel's *Heilsgeschichte* both set Egyptian bondage and Exodus at the heart of Israel's birth.[61] Both versions of the story of Samuel's installation of Saul set the institution of the monarchy in the light of the salvation from Egypt. The building of the Temple is twice discussed in reference to YHWH's not having required a house since the day he brought Israel out of Egypt (2 Sam. 7:6; 1 Kings 8:16), and the dedication of the Temple is dated to the year of the Exodus (1 Kings 6:1). Jeroboam is bound to identify his new cult with the "God(s) who brought you up out of the land of Egypt," (1 Kings 12:28). Even more telling are the numerous references to Egypt and the Exodus which are gratuitous to their immediate contexts (Deut. 4:45f.; 6:12; 8:14; 9:12; 13:6,11; 23:5; 24:9; 25:17; Judg. 2:12; 19:30; 2 Sam. 7:23; 1 Kings 8:51; 2 Kings 17:7). Egypt is plainly fundamental to the perspective of Dtr[1].

The perspective of the Exilic Deuteronomist is dramatically different from that of the earlier editor. The Exilic tradent focused above all on the people and not on the kings. The Exilic additions

---

[60] See also 16:1-3.

[61] Von Rad, "The Form-Critical Problem of the Hexateuch," in *The Problem of the Hexateuch*, pp. 3-8.

to the book of Deuteronomy of course have little to say of the monarch. The one reference seems to include the king only in passing, while the statement itself, threatening the curse of exile, is directed to the people (Deut. 28:36f.). All responsibility is placed upon the people in every Exilic passage. In the latter books, the Dtr[1] monarchical focus is deliberately redirected into a concern for the course of the nation. Thus the version of the Davidic promise which appears in 1 Kings 6:11-13 mentions no matters of dynastic security such as appear in the Dtr[1] passages, but promises that YHWH will not leave his people. The Exilic addition of 1 Kings 9:6-9 blatantly turns a specifically dynastic revelation to Solomon into a threatening warning to the people to keep the commandments. The inserted comment on the fall of Israel in 2 Kings 17:35-40a is not at all concerned with Jeroboam and his successors, but only with the failure of the children of Jacob to listen to YHWH. The Exilic prediction of the fall of Judah, set in the midst of the Dtr[1] reckoning of the crimes of Manasseh, places responsibility completely on the people, so that Manasseh, is blamed primarily as a catalyst. The issue, in Dtr[2], is much older than Manasseh. The nation is to suffer "because they did evil in my eyes and have been angering me from the day that their fathers went out of Egypt until this day," (2 Kings 21:15). The prophecy of Huldah (2 Kings 22:16f.) likewise has nothing to say about Manasseh or any other king. Only in two Exilic notices which follow the death of Josiah (23:26; 24:3f.) are the provocations of Manasseh an issue, but this is possible only because the Exilic tradent has already remodeled the Manasseh pericope as described. The whole of the post-Josiah record has little to say about the kings; as noted above, the kings are treated succinctly and nearly identically.

This concern for the people more than for the rulers is apparent in the matter of covenants as well. It is in the Exile that the tension between the Israelite covenant and the Davidic promise, which concerned Tsevat and Levenson, becomes critical. For the Exilic tradent, nonetheless, it is as if there were no dilemma at all. The Davidic promise is not mentioned, no theological justification of the abandonment of the commitment is attempted. Dtr[2] simply pulls the carpet out from under the feet of the Davidids. The last Davidic kings suffer the fate of their nation. The Dtr[2] - inserted curse in the book of Deuteronomy that "YHWH will send you and your king which you will set over you to a nation which you have not known. . ." (Deut. 28:36) realizes. Dtr[2] is only concerned with the covenant of YHWH and Israel.

34

The only indication of an interest in the future of the royal line lies in the final four verses of the work, noting the release of Jehoiachin from prison and maintenance in Babylon. This is, as Cross has observed, "a thin thread upon which to hand the expectations of the fulfillment of the promises to David."[62] These last verses in fact may not even be from the hand which produced the Dtr^2 edition, as will be discussed below. The tradent of Dtr^2 has sharpened the dreadful potentialities of the Israelite covenant in the book of Deuteronomy and has described their historical realization in 2 Kings. The Davidids are swallowed in the fate of the nation. The power of the tradition of their divine promise is simply·not recognized.

The Dtr^1 concern regarding apostasy is of course shared in Dtr^2. The difference is one of degree. In Dtr^2 'ĕlōhîm 'ăḥērîm is what the story is all about. It is the issue in nearly every Dtr^2 insertion. It is the cause of the downfall of the people.

Another shared theme of the two editions is that of testimony. Dtr^2 continues to develop the Dtr^1 concern that a properly witnessed warning has been given to Israel. The Exilic version, however, chooses new witnesses. In the Josianic version, the witness against Israel is the book of the Torah. "And it will be there as a witness against you," (Deut. 31:26). The problem for Dtr^2 is that its interests are not confined to the past, but rather look forward to restoration as well. The book's being *there* as a witness is less than inspiring after 587, when *there* no longer exists. The Exilic additions to Deuteronomy therefore repeatedly summon heaven and earth, eternal witnesses, to testify. The Song of Moses has thus provided Dtr^2 with an old revered foundation for any future promises.

Not to disregard the obvious, Exile is the primary concern of Dtr^2. The re-editing of the work was above all designed to explain the circumstance in which the Jews found themselves, and to begin to develop some notion of the course to take in the future. Almost all of Biblical scholarship relating to the Exile has focused on the portion of the community which was deported to Babylon. This is unfortunate, especially in the light of the Scriptural notations that only a very small fraction of the people was taken in the Babylonian deportations.[63] As noted above, Dtr^2 additions to Deuteronomy

---

[62] *CMHE*, p. 277.

[63] 4,600 by the reckoning of Jer. 52:28ff., approximately 11,600 in the light of 2

refer to the scattering (*hēpîṣ*) of the people. The number of refugees who fled to neighboring countries is unknown. The number of those who remained in Judah under the authority of the Babylonian appointee Gedaliah is unknown. Whatever the actual historical situation, however, there can be no doubt of the Exilic Deuteronomist's intended portrayal of the fate of the people. The final verse of the story of the people states:

> And all the people, young and old, and the officers of the soldiers arose and came to Egypt, for they feared the Babylonians.

> 2 Kings 25:26

This statement of the flight of the remnant of Israel to Egypt is an abbreviated version of the account in Jer. 43:4-7.

> But Johanan ben Kareah and all the officers of the soldiers and all the people did not listen to the voice of YHWH to live in the land of Judah. And Johanan ben Kareah and all the officers of the soldiers took all of the remnant of Judah which had returned from all the nations to which they had been driven to dwell in the land of Judah, the men and the women and the children and the daughters of the king and all the souls which Nebuzaradan, captain of the guard, had left with Gedaliah ben Ahikam ben Shaphan, and Jeremiah the prophet and Baruch ben Neriah. And they came to the land of Egypt, for they did not listen to the voice of YHWH, and they came to Tahpanhes.

So simply does the Deuteronomist report the extraordinary fate of the people that it simply has never been properly reckoned with in modern scholarship. The nation which was born in redemption from Egypt, and which was forbidden by Torah (Deut. 17:16) and prophet (Jeremiah 42) to return there, now seeks its security there. Now the horror of the final curse of Deuteronomy 28 can be understood:

Kings 24:14. Cf. Albright, *The Biblical Period from Abraham to Ezra*, p. 85; John Bright, *A History of Israel*, p. 345; A. Malamat, "The Twilight of Judah: In the Egyptian-Babylonian Maelstrom," *VTSup* 28 (1974), pp. 133f.

> And YHWH will cause you to return to Egypt in boats, in the way concerning which I said to you, "you will never see it again," and you will sell yourselves there to your enemies as slaves, and none will buy.

v. 68

The meaning of the reference to boats is an enigma. It may be an *aleflayin* scribal error for *ᶜnywt* (afflictions), though the form is unattested. It may be a form of the rare *'aniyāh* (mourning; cf. Isa. 29:2; Lam. 2:5), also unattested in the plural. It may refer to some historical circumstance. In any case, the concern with Egypt which pervades Dtr[1] becomes critical in the second edition. It raises the possibility that Dtr[2] is even a product of the Egyptian community, a possibility which is enhanced by the extreme similarity of style and interest between the Deuteronomistic history and the book of Jeremiah,[64] summoning to mind the Rabbinic claim of Jeremiah's authorship of the books of Kings.[65] This further raises the likelihood that the last four verses of the history (2 Kings 25:27-30), referring to the release of Jehoiachin, are not the work of Dtr[2], but are possibly the addition of a member of the Babylonian community. Whatever the situation with regard to authorship, the Deuteronomistic history, in its final form, tells the story of Israel from Egypt to Egypt.[66] It is the story of the failure of the covenant relations of YHWH and his people. The words of the old Song of Moses, "I shall hide my face from them, I shall see what their end will be," repeated and emphasized by the Exilic Deuteronomist (Deut. 31:17f.) in the mouth of Moses, now impose a direction upon the earlier edition of the history which points to YHWH's ultimate abandonment of his people.

> And my anger will burn at them in that day, and I shall leave them, and I shall hide my face from them, and they will be consumed, and many evils and troubles will find them, and they will say in that day, "Is it not because our God is not in our midst that these troubles have found us?"

---

[64] See above, n. 11.

[65] *Babylonian Talmud*, Tractate *Baba Batra* 15a.

[66] Jer. 44:1 identifies the places of settlement in Egypt as Tahpanhes, Noph, and the region of Pathros, all of which lay in the general area of the land of Goshen.

The predictions of Deuteronomy match the events of 2 Kings and so produce the image of a unified work, this image being enhanced by the very few, but artful, insertions in the body of the history. Dtr[2] thus over-encloses the inclusion of Dtr[1], and a story of hope and reform is revamped into an account of a people whose God abandons them to disaster. Our own next task is to uncover some of the thematic elements of each of the editions of the Deuteronomistic history which made this revamping and reconciliation of perspectives possible.

The insertion of a prediction that YHWH will one day hide his face, and of a fulfillment passage in which YHWH does turn Judah out "from before his face" (2 Kings 24:3), would not suffice to redirect an entire history of the relations of YHWH and his people unless elements of that original history which supported the notion of YHWH's leaving his people were already present. There is in fact a metamorphosis in the relations of YHWH and Israel through the course of the history which the Josianic tradent assembled. At several junctures the immanence of YHWH seems to diminish. Dtr[1] pictures Israel's early history as the events of an age of power, a time in which YHWH is seen to be clearly and regularly immanent in the life of the people, covenanting with them, appearing among them, and producing public miraculous events as signs and wonders. Nearly all of these marks of that age of power, however, begin to diminish early in Dtr[1] and completely disappear from the account early in the portrayal of the monarchy.

The simplest means of portraying an appearance of YHWH to an individual or community is through the *niphal* of the verb *r'h*, *to see*, which is properly translated *to appear* and connotes that YHWH, in some form, is actually seen. In Dtr[1] the term *wayyērā'* occurs in expression of a divine appearance via an angel to Manoah and his wife (Judg. 13:3,10f.,21) and to Gideon (Judg. 6:12). There is an unelaborated divine appearance to Samuel (1 Sam. 3:21) and to Solomon (1 Kings 9:2), and there is portrayed an appearance through dream to Solomon (1 Kings 3:5; 11:9). Solomon is the last Bibilical personage to whom YHWH is to have appeared. Following the second visitation to Solomon, the term *wayyera'* is never again employed in the Deuteronomist's narrative (nor in any other Biblical narrative).

A parallel term to *wayyērā'* is the *niphal* of the verb *glh*, which is also to be translated *to appear* or *to be revealed*. Its near synonymity with *wayyērā'* is indicated by a comparison of Gen. 35:1 and 35:7 (E) and by noting the juxtaposition of the two terms in 1

Sam. 3:21. In addition to the *nglh* appearance to Samuel, the historian recognizes that YHWH appeared in earlier times: "I surely appeared to your father's house when they were in Egypt in the house of Pharaoh," (1 Sam. 2:27).[67] But, as in the case of the term *wayyērā'*, the use of *nglh* ceases early in the Deuteronomistic history, the appearance to Samuel being the last case.

That which is pictured in the *kᵉbôd YHWH* is not certain. The term is generally translated *glory* and probably refers to the hypostatization of the abstract glory of YHWH.[68] The *kābôd* may be present in Israel or may leave, as indicated by 1 Sam. 4:21. The last appearance of the *kābôd* portrayed in Dtr[1] is on the occasion of the dedication of the Temple by Solomon, at which time the *kᵉbôd YHWH* is supposed to have filled YHWH's house (1 Kings 8:11). This is the last Biblical reference to the *kᵉbôd YHWH* as an actually present entity.[69]

The *ʿānān*, the cloud associated with YHWH's presence and in some way related to the *kābôd*, is also known until the time of Solomon.[70] At the dedication of the Temple, the priests are unable to minister because the cloud fills the Temple (1 Kings 8:10f.).[71] This is the last mention of the *ʿānān* in Dtr[1].

In addition to the foregoing expressions of the immanence of YHWH among his people, the tangible acts of YHWH via heavenly creatures and miraculous interventions arrives at a turning point very near the same juncture in the history. The last portrayal of an appearance of an angel is to the prophet Elijah (2 Kings 1:3,15). The one later mention of an angel, in the mysterious night calamity of the camp of Sennacherib in the seige of Jerusalem (2 Kings 19:35 = Isaiah 37:36), does not suggest the appearance of the *ml'k* nor does it suggest the angel's presence among the people of Israel.

---

[67] On the referent of this passage as Moses, see Julius Wellhausen, *Prolegomena to the History of Israel*, p. 142, (hereafter cited as *PHI*); and *CMHE*, pp. 196f.

[68] *CMHE*, pp. 153n., 165-167.

[69] Ezekiel sees the *kābôd* in a vision.

[70] Cross discusses the *ʿānān* together with the *kābôd*, *CMHE*, pp. 164-167. Cf. G. E. Mandenhall, *The Tenth Generation*, pp. 32-66.

[71] Mendenhall does not regard this passage as referring to the *ʿānān* of YHWH's presence, but rather as describing the smoke from the multitude of sacrifices, *The Tenth Generation*, p. 212. The text surely refers to the cloud of presence; I cannot see the justification of Mendenhall's interpretation. Cf. Exod. 40:34f.

The presence of YHWH as expressed through public miracles diminishes qualitatively and quantitatively. By public miracle is meant those miraculous events which are portrayed as occurring in the presence of and serving the well-being of the entire community of Israel or a significant portion thereof. Miracle is well-known in Dtr[1] and, in a certain respect, reaches a level beyond that of the Priestly work. The role attributed to Joshua personally in the miraculous halting of the sun (Josh. 10:12f.), for example, exceeds the degree to which even Moses and Aaron are portrayed as participating in the choice and the timing of signs and wonders. The text specially notes: "And there was no day like that before it or after it that YHWH hearkened to the voice of a man. . ." (v. 14). The control of miracles continues thereafter to fall increasingly into the hands of humans to a point at which YHWH deposits, as it were, a quantum of power at the disposal of a chosen man or woman who then controls the time, place, and drama of its use. Perhaps the clearest example of divine deposit of power in human control is the Samson narrative (Judg. 13-16), in which the man's might and the terms under which he retains it are set prenatally and surface thereafter in consequence of his personal activities, tastes, and weaknesses. Likewise, in the narrative of the duel of the prophets of YHWH and Baal on Mount Carmel (1 Kings 18), Elijah's speech, his mocking, his prayer, and his violent zeal all emphasize the role of Elijah personally in the event to an extent unmatched by perhaps any previous Biblical figure. To explain this as a stylistic difference between narrators is not sufficient. The difference is not merely one of character development; it is rather of the degree to which a human participates in and controls the miraculous event, divine control decreasing inversely. Without denying that YHWH continues to be the source of the power behind miracle, one observes that in Dtr[1], in a qualitative sense, his role diminishes. This phenomenon reaches its extreme level in the personal miracles of Elijah and especially of Elisha, in which the prophets are apparently in full control of power, using it as they please.

From a quantitative perspective as well, analysis of public (as opposed to personal) miracle points to the diminishing immanence of YHWH. Occurrences of miracle generally are a measure of the presence of YHWH in Israel. Particularly interesting in this regard is the remark of Gideon, "If YHWH is present with us why has all this befallen us ($m^e s\bar{a}'atn\hat{u}$) and where are all his wonders of which our fathers told us saying 'Did not YHWH bring us up from Egypt,' but now YHWH has forsaken us," (Judg. 6:13). Public miracle is regarded as a sign of the presence of YHWH. The last public miracle in Dtr[1] is that of Elijah on Mount Carmel. The miraculous deeds of Elisha which follow are personal, smaller, indeed petty by comparison, in purpose and audience. Whatever the significance of the she-bears' devouring of the brats (2 Kings 2:23f.) or of the recovery of the axehead (6:1-7) or even of the revival of the dead child (4:18-37), their importance and impact cannot match the event on Carmel.

The cessation of the great public miracles which play a significant role in the birth, preservation, and development of Israel falls therefore in the Deuteronomist's narrative of the events of the ninth century, i.e., shortly subsequent to the section in which the chief terminology of divine presence ceases. The accounts of the monarchies which follow lack wholly the conveyed sense of YHWH's immanence among his people which pervades the preceding books. One clearly senses that the age of power is past. Though the text continues to regard YHWH as affecting history as a behind-the-scenes motivator, he is himself no longer an actor, his presence no longer portrayed.

It is interesting to note that, after the account of Elijah at Carmel, is inserted the account of Elijah at Horeb (1 Kings 19). This story is probably related to the Yahwistic account of Moses at Sinai.[72] The prophet goes to the place of his predecessor's closest revelation of YHWH and greatest personal moment. But to Elijah is not given a comparable experience of the divine presence. On the contrary, each of the phenomena formerly associated with theophany (wind, quake, fire) is marked by the notation: YHWH was not in it; and all are followed by a sound of thin hush.[73] YHWH's first words to Elijah thereafter are, "What business have you here, Elijah?" The time of direct revelation of the presence of YHWH is past, a face-to-face stage of Israel's story is replaced by one which is more properly a stage of approaching divine hiddenness, and the story which conveys this change so pointedly is inserted at precisely the juncture in the Deuteronomistic history at which the language of divine presence and the portrayal of public miraculous phenomena cease.

---

[72] *CMHE*, p. 166.

[73] Cross has emphasized the importance of this scene as a turning from expressions of YHWH's activity through the Baalesque language of the storm theophany. "The abrupt refusal of YHWH to appear as in the traditional theophany at Sinai marked the beginning of a new era in his mode of self-disclosure." *CMHE*, pp. 193f.

The narrative which follows portrays the further deterioration of relations between YHWH and the two kingdoms. In the course of this narrative, to the end of Dtr[1], YHWH never again speaks directly to a king or to the people. The manner in which he communicates with prophets is not portrayed. The one channel to YHWH which Dtr[1] continues to develop, referring to it as late as the Manasseh pericope, is the Deuteronomistic Name theology, which, as discussed above, relates to the survival of the Temple as a channel to a transcendent God. Even in this matter, nonetheless, the context of the last reference is hardly positive. The wording of the reference to the Name theology in the Manasseh narrative is ironic and foreboding:

> And he set a statue of Asherah which he had made in
> the house of which YHWH had said to David and to
> Solomon his son, "In this house and in Jerusalem which
> I have chosen from all the tribes of Israel I shall set my
> Name forever.

2 Kings 21:7

The Dtr[1] edition of the history thus concludes in a state of things which seems far removed from the age of Moses, a fact which seems to be more underscored than reversed by the associations drawn between Moses and Josiah. The ancient age of power seems to be the age of authority as well, and the task of the Josianic age is portrayed as one of obedience to the authority of the book which the former era produced.

It is difficult to say whether the author/editor of Dtr[1] consciously developed this metamorphosis in the relations of YHWH and humans. It is certainly due in part to the combination of varying genres of the sources, in part to the varying temporal distances between authors and their subjects, in part to what seems to be a common human feeling that ages of power stand behind us. This last factor, in Israel, would manifest itself in a feeling that the nation is moving ever further from the extraordinary characters and events of the days of its youth. This development will receive attention in the coming chapter. In any event, there can be no doubt that the ultimate break between YHWH and the people of Israel was a conscious development in the work of the Exilic tradent. The diminishing apparent presence of YHWH in Dtr[1] suited the work of Dtr[2] perfectly. The predictions of the disaster to come which Dtr[2] adds to the Manasseh pericope and to the Huldah prophecy fit their contexts well. When Dtr[2] devastates the Name theology in the Exilic conclusion to the history (2 Kings 23:27),[74] the last channel to YHWH is severed. The final edition of the history thus tells the story of the relations of YHWH and the people, deteriorating from their first acquaintance until the final abandonment of the people, "cast from before my face," in Exile.

Another of the interests of Dtr[2] which reconciled naturally with the interests of the received edition was the compassion of YHWH as a source of hope for restoration. As discussed above, the Exilic insertion of Deut. 4:25-31 modified a context of a fiery, threatening jealous God, *'ēl qannā'*, by adding comforting words of hope that a compassionate God, *'ēl raḥûm*, would not forget his covenant with the fathers. Such a reversal, like the promise of restoration and plenty in the Exilic Deut. 30:1-10, was possible because the portrayal of YHWH both as angry and as compassionate deity had been developed through the course of the writing of the Josianic tradent and of his sources. Not only are the terms *rḥm* and *qn'* in use in the Dtr[1] edition (Deut. 4:24; 5:9; 6:15; 13:18; 29:19; II Sam. 24:14; I Kings 14:22; II Kings 13:23), but more to the point, the two themes are regularly and crucially bound into the fabric of the narrative. The Deuteronomistic introduction to the stories of the judges (Judg. 2:11-23) illustrates this well, portraying Israel as alternately arousing the anger and the mercies of YHWH, setting this pattern as the *Leitmotif* of the old accounts which follow, thus:

> And the anger of YHWH burned against Israel. . . and he sold them into the hand of their enemies. . . Wherever they went the hand of YHWH was against them for harm. . . and they were greatly distressed. . . And when YHWH raised up judges for them YHWH was with the judge and saved them from the hand of their enemies all the days of the judge, for YHWH relented because of their cry before their oppressors and persecutors. And it came to pass that at the death of the judge they returned and corrupted themselves more than their fathers to go after other gods. . . they did not cease from their deeds and from their hard way. And the anger of YHWH burned against Israel. . .

---

[74] See above, pp. 10-12.

This vacillating balance between the extremes of the feelings of YHWH toward his people also informs the prayer of Solomon on the occasion of the dedication of the Temple. This Deuteronomistic composition presumes the eventuality of the people's offense and YHWH's angry response, and the prayer thus turns to appeal to his compassion and forgiveness. A show of humility by an Israelite or Judean king can likewise arouse these feelings in YHWH and thus postpone a decree of chastisement, not only in a king such as Josiah (2 Kings 22:19f.), but even from such a berated ruler as Ahab (1 Kings 21:29). It is likewise the compassion of YHWH and his memory of his covenant with the fathers which preserves Israel from the Syrian oppression under Hazael (2 Kings 13:23).

The presence of this development in Dtr[1] rendered it possible for the Exilic tradent to portray the bitterest of accounts of wrath and chastisement together with the bright promises of a return and bounteous restoration. The Exilic Deuteronomist redirected the received work and was responsible for producing the narrative which we read. The perspective of the Deuteronomistic history is that of this Exilic figure, as is the climax of the work. This monumental literary transformation of the character of the Deuteronomistic history was possible, however, only because the theological and historical traditions which were already present in the received edition were eminently suitable as a foundation upon which to develop the Exilic concerns. Those interests which were common to the two editions yielded a unity which further enhanced the literary merger. Those interests include concern for the Israelite covenant, the establishment of witness concerning the nation's survival and well-being, utter rejection of other gods, Egypt, and Torah. The final product, molded under the impact of Exile, is the story of the middle era of the Biblical account of Israel, from Egypt to Egypt. The Priestly account of the prior era is the concern of the next chapter.

Chapter II

The Impact of Exile on the Character of the

Priestly Work

I. That there were two principal stages of the Priestly work, the first in response to the Josianic edition of the Deuteronomistic history (Dtr[1]), the second Exilic.

Identification and separation of the Priestly components of the Torah from the JE sources is a less subtle task than identification and separation of Dtr[2] from Dtr[1]. Unlike the enterprise of the Exilic Deuteronomist, the Priestly materials were not composed in conscious stylistic imitation of older work and are generally not difficult to distinguish.[1] The more perplexing task of Pentateuchal literary analysis has been internal to P, namely to determine what portion of P is an Exilic (or post-Exilic) product, and to explain the relationship of P to JE and Deuteronomistic materials. The locus of P relative to 587 has been precisely the prime issue between the two schools of thinking in Biblical scholarship which are identified with the works of Julius Wellhausen and Yehezkel Kaufmann.[2] Wellhausen's assignment of the Priestly source primarily to the post-Exilic period depended above all on the attitude toward the centralization of worship which he perceived in that source. He saw the Priestly requirement that all sacrifice take place at the Tabernacle (*miškān*) as expressing the same expectation of centralized worship as the Deuteronomic[3] requirement that all sacrifice take place at "the place where YHWH will set his name."[4] The distinction lay in the observation that D *demanded* this centralization, consistent with the Josianic reform of which D was a part, while P *presumed* that centralized worship was normative, consistent with a time when the Josianic demand was an accepted, institutionalized

---

[1] My source identifications are collected in the Appendix.

[2] Wellhausen, *PHI*; Kaufmann, *twldwt h'mwnh hyśr'lyt,* English edition: *The Religion of Israel*, trans., Moshe Greenberg, (hereafter cited as *RI*).

[3] See above, Chapter I, n. 11.

[4] See above, Chapter I, n. 17.

reality—namely: the Second Temple period. The Tabernacle, its structure, and its laws represent the Second Temple and are a literary device designed to summon Mosaic authority without anachronism. Other P elements likewise seemed to reflect this period, notably the distinction between priests and Levites, which was absent in the undifferentiated notion of "Levitical priests" in D. The separation of the holidays from their original natural/agricultural orientation, as well, seemed to fit the late period; the Autumnal New Year and Day of Atonement, whose emphasis upon guilt and repentance Wellhausen interpreted as a response to the destruction and Exile, particularly pointed to late composition.

Kaufmann objected to Wellhausen's notion of the Tabernacle as a model of the Second Temple, noting first that several features of the two were not comparable: the ark, cherubim, *urim* and *tummim* of the Tabernacle had no reflexes in the Temple. Specifically with regard to centralization of worship, Kaufmann noted that the Deuteronomic demand that all sacrificial slaughter be performed at the chosen place is accompanied by explicit permission to perform non-ritual slaughter anywhere (Deut. 12:15ff.). The Priestly laws contain no such permission. If the Priestly Tabernacle corresponds to the Second Temple, Kaufmann argued, then no one who lived outside of Jerusalem could have eaten meat except with considerable pains. Rather, in Kaufmann's view, the Priestly Tabernacle must correspond to the local sanctuaries of numerous Israelite towns, it reflects the opposite of centralization, and P therefore was composed prior to the Josianic reform. The absence in the Priestly source of any recognition of the Deuteronomic festival pilgrimage law also seemed to Kaufmann to be inexplicable if the composition of P was later than Josiah. He also argued that the Priestly treatment of the Paschal sacrifice (Exod. 12:2-20) prescribes a home sacrifice and that this, too must pre-date centralization. Kaufmann rejected the Wellhausenian treatment of the festivals, pointing to the festivals of Israel's neighbors which quite early knew fixity in times and rites rather than the required natural spontaneity of the view of Wellhausen; and Kaufmann understood the New Year and Day of Atonement to be festivals of purification, not oriented towards guilt at all. Kaufmann argued, further, that the priest/Levite distinction pre-dated Josiah, was lost during the late pre-Exilic days of D, and was reborn after Exile. P therefore, according to Kaufmann, is older than D.

Beyond the question of the historical relationship of the Pentateuchal sources, recent scholarship has focused increasingly upon their literary relationship. With Noth's identification of the Deuteronomistic history, discussed in Chapter I, he has drawn the complementary conclusion that the Priestly work was properly the Tetrateuch and did not extend into a Hexateuch.[5] Noth has suggested further that P is primarily a narrative source, the work of a single author (plus supplements), and is the normative literary basis of the work, i.e. P is the favored *Grundlage* of the redactor, and "Generally speaking it can be expected that only the P narrative is preserved completely in its original extent and that therefore the identified P elements connect smoothly with each other—something which, contrariwise, cannot be said in every case for the narrative which rests on the old sources."[6] Noth has also remarked that the extent to which the Priestly narrative parallels that of JE, both in sequence and particulars, suggests that P drew the narrative material from those sources.[7] Sigmund Mowinckel has provided a more thorough demonstration of this relationship in a careful comparison of P with JE at each unit of their respective accounts.[8] Mowinckel has restrained his conclusion to a cautious statement that P depended "directly or indirectly" upon the older source. Cross, however, has suggested that the relationship of the Priestly and JE materials is integral. As opposed to Noth's view of P as an independent narrative source which a redactor enriched with JE additions, Cross has argued that P was never an independent source and is not properly narrative.[9] Separated from JE, the narrative of P is scant in the book of Genesis—a fact acknowledged by Mowinckel—with only the Flood and Machpelah accounts worthy of the term. P appears to Cross (as it did to Wellhausen) to be more a framework housing older sources than a source itself (though Wellhausen did not go on to question its original

---

[5] Noth, *UGS*. Kaufmann and Engnell also regarded Genesis-Numbers and Deuteronomy-Kings as the appropriate literary categories; each of the three scholars arrived at this observation independently. Kaufmann, *RI*, p. 205; Engnell, *A Rigid Scrutiny*, pp. 58f.

[6] Noth, *A History of Pentateuchal Traditions*, p. 17, (hereafter cited as *HPT*).

[7] *HPT*, p. 234.

[8] Mowinckel, *Erwägungen zur Pentateuch Quellenfrage*, pp. 26-43. See also Sean E. McEvenue, *The Narrative Style of the Priestly Writer*.

[9] *CMHE*, chap. 11.

independence). Particularly telling is the absence of elements which, Cross emphasizes, one would expect to be crucial to the Priestly scheme. These include the absence of any development of the birth of corruption in the otherwise "exceeding good" Creation comparable to that of J (Gen. 3; 4; 6:1-5) and the absence of any introduction or youth-account of Moses, who appears out of nowhere (Exod. 6:2) with a mission to end an oppression which P has not yet mentioned. But the loudest of the silences of P, Cross notes, is the absence of the covenant-making at Sinai. Cross has thus described the Tetrateuch as the product of a Priestly tradent (Exilic) whose task, not unlike that of the Deuteronomistic historians, was the assembly of received texts (including JE, the Covenant Code, the Holiness Code and other pre-Exilic Priestly compositions), expanded by material of his own composition within a framework which he constructed out of still other received texts, specifically the *tôlᵉdōt* book and the Wilderness Stations list of Numbers 33. This tradent replaces the posited unknown redactor of classical criticism.

Ivan Engnell has likewise understood the Priestly work not as a single narrative source, but rather has spoken in terms of a P "circle" (Exilic or post-Exilic) which was responsible for assembling older P materials, as well as JE materials, into the Tetrateuch.[10] Some of the Priestly materials, in Engnell's view, are of great antiquity. Like Kaufmann, Engnell has remarked that P seems to have no interest in centralization, though Engnell has understood the Tabernacle traditions to derive from the pre-Jerusalemite period rather than to symbolize local sanctuaries.

In order to pursue the literary issue which is central to the views of Cross and Noth, one must necessarily return first to the question of the historical relationship of the sources. The Wellhausen/Kaufman issue of what portion of P is pre-Exilic and what portion Exilic or post-Exilic, as we shall see, is critical to this task.

The Priestly portrayal of the Tabernacle is all-important. In the Torah, more attention is devoted to this structure than to any other subject. According to the Priestly accounts, from the day of the Tabernacle dedication all revelation occurs there, all sacrifice, all burning of incense, all priestly consumption of offerings (in its

---

[10] Engnell, *A Rigid Scrutiny*, p. 58. This book is a translation of several of the articles which Engnell contributed to *Svenskt Bibliskt Uppslagsverk*, which he edited.

48

court); it houses the covenant tablets, the ark, the cherubim; it is constructed of precious wood, metals, and fabrics according to divine instruction; only the priests may enter it; only the high priests may enter its Holy of Holies.

One must acknowledge that very little of the Tabernacle description has any reflex in the Second Temple. Even with regard to dimensions, the Tabernacle is not proportionate either to the First Temple or to Ezekiel's plan for the Second Temple. Still, the Priestly description corresponds even less satisfactorily to the local places of worship in pre-Josianic Israel and Judah, for which the discussion of ark, cherubs, *urim* and *tummim*, and high priests has no relevance.

Let us weigh an alternative proposal beside the suggestions of Wellhausen and Kaufmann, namely that the Priestly Tabernacle is neither a symbolic representation of the Second Temple nor of the local sanctuaries, but, not a symbol, *the Priestly Tabernacle refers to the historical Tabernacle, which was located in the First Temple.* The Biblical histories report explicitly that the Tent of Assembly was brought up to the Temple of Solomon on the day of the Temple dedication, together with the ark and the sanctified vessels (1 Kings 8:4 = 2 Chron. 5:5), but this verse has, since Wellhausen, been regarded as a gloss because of the infrequent references to the Tabernacle in the history of the land prior to this report[11]. This is hardly sufficient grounds for pronouncing a gloss, especially in light of our present understanding of the Deuteronomistic history as a composite work, which demands caution in the use of such a contextual argument—most of the material in the two books which precede the Solomon material is, after all, derived from a separate document, the Court History of David. Menahem Haran has argued that 1 Kings 8:4 is a Priestly insertion,[12] though a

[11] Wellhausen, *PHI*, p. 43.

[12] Menahem Haran, "Shiloh and Jerusalem: The Origin of the Priestly Tradition in the Pentateuch," *JBL* 81 (1962), p. 21; cf. Virgil Rabe, "The Identity of the Priestly Tabernacle," *JNES* 25 (1966), pp. 132-134. See most recently Haran, *Temples and Temple-Service in Ancient Israel*, pp. 141n., 200. Haran also holds that the Tabernacle is not merely an artificial projection of a solid building (pp. 195ff.). (In the reference to "the priests *and* the Levites" in 1 Kings 8:4, the conjunction is contrary to the regular Deuteronomistic "Levitical Priests" notion. As the Greek text, however, lacks the conjunction, the *waw* in the MT is not sufficient evidence of a secondary addition here.)

forthcoming monograph by Baruch Halpern makes a new case for the originality of this verse to the historians' source. In any event, I shall argue here for the validity of the report of the arrival of the Tabernacle at the Temple regardless of the literary stage at which that report entered the narrative. One must be more willing to recognize the validity of the report of the Deuteronomist and of the Chronicler, moreover, when one examines the dimensions of the Tabernacle. As we have already observed, these dimensions are by no reckoning proportionate to those of either Temple. In the standard estimates the Tabernacle, as described in the book of Exodus, is thirty cubits in length, ten in width, and ten in height.[13] The First Temple, as described in 1 Kings 6, is sixty cubits in length, twenty in width, and thirty in height. It is thus three times the height of the Tabernacle but twice its length and width. Claims of correspondence of the dimensions of the Tabernacle with the Second Temple are completely groundless, as the dimensions of the Second Temple are not reported anywhere in the Hebrew Bible.[14] The measurements of the Tabernacle correspond rather to those of the space inside the Holy of Holies in the First Temple, beneath the wings of the cherubim. According to the description of the Temple construction (1 Kings 6; 2 Chronicles 3) the Holy of Holies (or *dᵉbîr*) is twenty cubits in length and twenty cubits in width (1 Kings 6:20; 2 Chron. 3:8). Within are the two cherubim, each ten cubits high. Their wings are spread (unlike most extant examples[15]), and the wingspread of each is ten cubits, so that the tips of the wings of each touch the walls of the room on each side and touch each other in the center of the room (1 Kings 6:23-27; 2 Chron. 3:10-13). Thus the space between the cherubim is ten cubits in height, twenty cubits in length, and less than ten cubits in width (as the bodies of the cherubim take up a portion of the

---

[13] References below. In my own calculation, the Tabernacle is twenty cubits in length, eight in width, ten in height. Neither calculation corresponds to either Temple.

[14] According to Ezra 6:3 Cyrus had directed that the Second Temple be constructed sixty cubits high and 60 cubits in breadth. There is no report concerning whether this direction was followed; and, again, the Tabernacle dimensions do not correspond.

[15] See W.F. Albright, "What were the Cherubim?" *BAR* I (1961), pp. 95-97; G. Ernest Wright, *Biblical Archeology*, pp. 137-142. See also the illustration in Th. A. Busink, *Der Temple von Jerusalem*, p. 198. The wings are generally folded back along the body of the cherub.

center space). The measurements of the Tabernacle, as pictured in Exodus 26 and 36, are just this: ten cubits in height, twenty cubits in length, and eight cubits in width. Scholars have hitherto reckoned the Tabernacle dimensions differently owing to the manner in which the Tabernacle construction is portrayed in the book of Exodus.[16] The exact measurements are never stated outright but must be derived from the description of the materials and structure. The Tabernacle is constructed of forty-eight wooden frames, each ten cubits long and a cubit-and-a-half wide. There are twenty frames in each of the two long sides of the Tabernacle and eight frames in the rear (western) wall.[17] The Tabernacle has thus been judged to be thirty cubits in length, ten cubits in width, and ten cubits in height.[18] The First Temple, as noted above, is sixty cubits in length, twenty in width, and thirty in height; and scholars have noted the two-to-one proportional correspondence between Temple and Tabernacle.[19] The heights of the two, however, do not thus correspond, being rather three-to-one; and the ten-cubit width of the Tabernacle, after all, is merely a guess, formulated with the Temple measurements in mind. One might ask, further, why the unusual cubit-and-a-half measurement is required for the frames rather than, for example, thirty frames of a cubit's width on each side of the Tabernacle. One must also question the assumption that the frames stand "shoulder-to-shoulder," i.e. each standing with its long edge flush against that of the next frame (see Figure 1) rather than, for example overlapping one another (see Figure 2). The latter in fact seems the more likely in light of the instruction that five rods hold these frames together on each side of the Tabernacle, the middle rod extending "in the midst of" (*btwk*) the frames (Exod. 26:28).[20] If the frames overlap one another by a half cubit,

---

[16] Cf. A.R.S. Kennedy, "Tabernacle," *Hastings Dictionary of the Bible*, IV, pp. 653-668; Cross, "The Priestly Tabernacle," *BA* 10 (1947), pp. 45-68, reprinted in *BAR* I (1961), pp. 201-228; Haran, "The Priestly Image of the Tabernacle," *HUCA* 36 (1965), pp. 191-226. For further bibliography of literature on the Tabernacle construction, see Haran, *Temples and Temple Service*, p. 150n.

[17] The arrangement of the eight frames is particularly difficult to determine as the two end frames are somehow specially set to support the corners of the structure (Exod. 26:22-25; 36:27-30).

[18] Haran, "The Priestly Image of the Tabernacle," pp. 192ff.

[19] Rabe, "The Temple as Tabernacle," (Harvard dissertation, 1963), p. 66, and references.

[20] I am advised that this arrangement is also structurally more sound than the

then the twenty-frame length and eight-frame width result in a structure which is twenty by eight cubits.[21]

The measurements of the fabric which encloses the frames verify these dimensions. It is a doubled layer of linen cloth, each half of which is composed of five curtains sewn together. Each curtain is twenty-eight cubits in length and four cubits in width, and so the five-curtain pieces are then joined by a set of fifty gold rings which attach to loops along their length. When this fabric is folded in half to form a double layer and spread over the frames, the gold rings surround the entrance (eastern side) of the Tabernacle. The twenty-cubit width of the fabric matches the twenty-cubit length of the Tabernacle. The twenty-eight cubit length of the fabric also matches perfectly the area which it covers, i.e. it extends over each of the ten-cubit-high walls of the Tabernacle and across the eight-cubit-wide ceiling (see Figure 4). This tends to confirm the twenty-by-eight-by-ten arrangement of the frames suggested above. One may of course question whether the curtains actually extend to the ground on either side of the Tabernacle. This doubt may be put to rest, however, when one observes that a second fabric is spread over the first. This outer fabric is likewise composed of paired sets of curtains, in this case united and doubled with brass rings instead of gold. This fabric differs from the first in that its component curtains are all thirty cubits long instead of twenty-eight (Exod. 26:8), and the text specifically refers to the extra cubit which is left on each side, which is to be folded back against the Tabernacle (26:13).

Further confirmation that the structure is eight cubits in width may be deduced from another difference between the inner fabric (referred to as the miškān) and the outer fabric (referred to as the 'ōhel). The outer fabric is composed of eleven curtains rather than ten. This leaves an extra four cubit-wide curtain falling back upon the rear (western) wall (mwl pny h'hl, Exod. 26:9). When folded over the rear wall, the two four-cubit sides of this curtain add up to an eight-cubit wide envelope upon the Tabernacle (26:12; see Figure 5).

Against this arrangement, one may object that it requires that the gold and brass rings surround the entrance of the Tabernacle

"flush" arrangement with regard to stability.

[21] Or twenty-and-a-half by eight-and-a-half, depending on the arrangement of the corner frames. See suggested arrangement, Figure 3.

while the Masoretic Text declares that the veil (*pārōket*) which divides the interior of the Tabernacle into two chambers (the Holy, and the Holy of Holies) is to be hung "under the rings" (Exod. 26:33) and thus requires that the rings be further back from the entrance.[22] Against this objection, one must note, first, that the *Septuagint* text of this verse calls for a reading of "under the frames" (translating Hebrew *qᵉrāsîm*) rather than the MT "under the rings" (Hebrew: *qᵉrāsîm*). Second, one must doubt whether the *pārōket* is a hanging veil at all. The text rather suggests that it is a pavilion (*sukkāh*) which covers the place of the ark inside the Tabernacle. It hangs upon four columns. YHWH commands Moses, "And you shall make the *pārōket* cover (*wᵉsakkōtā*) over the ark," (Exod. 40:3). It is referred to as the *pārōket hammāsāk* (Exod. 40:21; Num. 4:5). Two passages outside of the Priestly description use the term *sukkāh* in Tabernacle contexts (Ps. 27:5; Lam. 2:6). Indeed, since in the Rabbinic period the term had come to be accepted as meaning *veil*, the Rabbis strained at the wording of the Biblical text, thus:

> 'And you shall make the *pārōket* cover over the ark.' The *pārōkèt* was a partition, yet the Scriptures call it a covering (*skkh*). Consequently, a partition is meant in the sense of a covering. And the Rabbis (explain it thus): It means that it is bent a little (at the top) so that it looks like a covering.[23]

The Rabbis' difficulty with the text dramatizes the problematic character of the view of the *pārōket* as a veil. It is apparently a pavilion. It thus can hardly be spoken of as standing under the line of gold rings, and so we must prefer the *Septuagint* reading, regarding the *pārōket* as erected under the level of the frames as a housing for the ark.

---

[22] Cf. the specifications of Kennedy and Haran, which call for a thirty-cubit length and do not fold the fabric into a double layer, thus dividing the structure at the point of the rings into a twenty-cubit Holy place and a ten-cubit Holy of Holies. (The problem remains in this arrangement that rings of gold and brass are not visible from inside or outside the structure.)

[23] *Babylonian Talmud*, Tractate *Sukkah* 7b; see also Tractate *Soṭah* 37a and *Menaḥot* 62a, 98a; since Exod. 40:3 requires that the *pārōket* be set ᶜ*al* the ark, the *Gemara* here concludes that Hebrew ᶜ*al* means "near to!"

The Tabernacle thus is not a scale reflex of either Temple. It does however fit the place where the ark is set in 1 Kings 8 = 2 Chronicles 5, beneath the wings of the cherubim in the Holy of Holies of the First Temple.

The Chronicler's history offers further evidence that the historians pictured the Tabernacle as necessarily located in the Temple. The Deuteronomistic history, on the one hand, records the fact that in David's time the ark is set "in its place, in the tent, which David had pitched for it" (2 Sam. 6:17). It is not clear whether this tent is supposed to be the venerated tent of old (of Shiloh? of Moses?) or a new tent constructed by David.[24] The Chronicler, on the other hand, takes special pains to distinguish between two tents. In the Chronicler's version, David appoints Levites and priests to remain at the tent which houses the ark in Jerusalem (1 Chron. 16:1-6, 37f.), but he sends Zadok and his retinue to conduct the regular sacrifices at the Tabernacle of YHWH which is located at the *bāmāh* of Gibeon, "to offer burnt offerings to YHWH on the altar of burnt offerings continually, morning and evening, and according to all that is written in the Torah of YHWH which he commanded upon Israel" (16:39f.). The Chronicler thus understands the Tabernacle to be the place at which the Priestly laws of daily sacrifice are to be executed, taking priority even over the place where the ark is housed. Thus the Deuteronomistic history records an occasion on which Solomon "went to Gibeon to sacrifice there because it was the great *bāmāh*" (1 Kings 3:4). The Deuteronomist added a critical note, v. 3, faulting Solomon for sacrificing at *bāmôt*. The Chronicler's history, however, records the same event thus:

> Solomon and all the congregation with him went to the *bāmāh* which is in Gibeon because the Tent of Meeting of God, which Moses the servant of YHWH had made in the wilderness, was there; but the ark of God David

---

[24] It is not necessary here to enter upon the historical question of the origin of the Tabernacle, concerning which cf. Cross, "The Priestly Tabernacle," pp. 221ff., who argues that the P traditions reflect the Davidic tent; and Haran, "Shiloh and Jerusalem," pp. 20-24, who argues that they reflect the Shiloh structure. My concern at this particular point is the literary question of the portrayed origin and location of the Tabernacle.

had brought up from Kiriath-Yearim into the (place which) David had prepared for it, for he had pitched a tent for it in Jerusalem.

(2 Chron. 1:3f.)

Again the Chronicler understood the Tabernacle (or Tent of Meeting) to be the proper setting of sacrifice, as declared in P. The pejorative Dtr notation regarding Solomon's sacrificing at bāmôt is thus missing in the Chronicler's version. The Chronicler manifestly favored the Tabernacle over the place of the ark as the locus of commanded worship. Thus the Chronicler took pains to explain that David's sacrifice at the threshing floor of Ornan was permissible despite the fact that the Tabernacle was at Gibeon (1 Chron. 21:28-30).

One may note one more reflection of this difference between the Deuteronomist and Chronicler in the wording of the prophet Nathan's oracle to David. In the Deuteronomist's version YHWH declares that he has always gone about b'hl wbmškn ("in tent and in Tabernacle," 2 Sam. 7:6). This can be construed to be a single structure, for, as noted above, the Tent of Meeting is composed of an inner fabric which is referred to as miškān and an outer fabric which is referred to as 'ōhel,[25] or it may be a hendiadys. The Chronicler's version, however, leaves no doubt of the plurality of the structures, declaring that YHWH has gone about "from tent to tent, and from Tabernacle" (1 Chron. 17:5, Hebrew text). This unusual wording is more than just a "break-up" of the hendiadys in 2 Sam. 7:6.[26] It corresponds to the Chronicler's actual historical portrayal, in which the ark has in fact moved "from tent to tent," namely: from the Tent of Meeting to the Tent of David. But the ark cannot be spoken of as having moved "from Tabernacle to Tabernacle," because only the structure within the Tent of Meeting is properly called the Tabernacle. David's Tent is never referred to as the Tabernacle. Thus the Chronicler says: "from tent to tent, and from Tabernacle." (The Greek translator apparently did not perceive this historical connection.) Thus the portrayal of the transfer of the Tent of Meeting to Jerusalem in 2 Chron. 5:5 is

---

[25] Cf. Num. 3:25.

[26] On the Biblical techniques of hendiadys and "break-up," see Shemaryahu Talmon's treatment, "The Textual Study of the Bible — A New Outlook," in Cross and Talmon, eds., Qumran and the History of the Biblical Text, pp. 321-400.

crucial to the Chronicler's portrayal of history; the Tabernacle must be in the Temple of Solomon in order to establish the Temple as Israel's legitimate place of worship. In the Deuteronomist's account, the tent which David pitches is either regarded as the successor of the Tent of Meeting or as the Tent of Meeting itself. In either case, the Deuteronomist and chronicler are solidly agreed on one fact: Solomon brings the Tent of Meeting up with the ark on the day of the dedication of the Temple.

Another reference to the presence of the Tent of Meeting inside the First Temple appears in a list of Davidic appointments in an extremely complex chapter of the Chronicler's history (1 Chron. 9:19-23). The list refers to gatekeepers at the entrance of the Tent of Meeting (9:19,21) and concludes:

whm wbnyhm ʿl hšʿrym

lbyt yhwh lbyt h'hl lmšmrwt

And they and their sons were over the gates *of the House of YHWH, the House of the Tent,* in watches.

Here the Temple is explicitly referred to as "the House of YHWH, the House of the Tent." And this House of the Tent realizes the succession of the Tent of Meeting.[27]

A reference to the Tabernacle appears also in the Chronicler's account of the reform of Hezekiah (2 Chronicles 29). In this pericope, Hezekiah addresses the priests and Levites, instructing them to clean and sanctify the House of YHWH because of the trespasses of Judah against YHWH and his Temple. He declares:

---

[27] One might argue that the wording "the House of YHWH, the House of the Tent" is rather the result of scribal errors in copying. The phrase "the House of YHWH," after all, does not occur elsewhere in this section (1 Chron. 9:1-34), but rather "the House of God (*'lhym*)." One might suggest a scribal error here in which *byt h'hl* (the House of the Tent) was substituted for the similarly-spelled *byt h'lhym* (the House of God). I would respond that such a suggestion calls for too complex a scribal process. Beyond the error of *h'hl* for *h'lhym*, one must also picture a second change, in which a scribe made an interlinear correction and, for some reason, chose to correct with the phrase *byt yhwh* instead of *byt h'lhym*. One must then picture a third change, in which a scribe copied both the error and the correction. While this general type of error does occasionally occur, this particular example seems excessively speculative, especially in light of the numerous other tent references cited here.

". . . they turned their faces from the Tabernacle of
YHWH and turned their backs, they also shut the doors
of the hall ('ûlām) and put out the lamps, and they did
not burn incense nor offer burnt offerings in the holy
(place) to the God of Israel."

(29:6b,7)

The reference to the Tabernacle hardly seems to be meant figura-
tively here in a list of offenses against specific Temple accoutre-
ments and functions. The Chronicler portrayed the Tabernacle as
located in the Temple.

In the similar remarks of Joash to the priests, the Chronicler's
account differs from that of the Deuteronomist (2 Kings 12:8),
again, in a reference to the Tent (2 Chron. 24:6).

In 1 Chron. 6:16f., there is a reference to David's appointment of individuals to serve before miškān 'ōhel môʿēd "until
Solomon built the house of YHWH." The list of their names then
concludes with a reference to the Levites as serving before the
miškān bêt ha'elōhîm (6:33)!

The service of the Levites with regard to the Tent of Meeting
and with regard to the Aaronid priests is tied specifically to the bêt
YHWH again in 1 Chron. 23:32.

The books of Chronicles thus consistently picture the Tabernacle as housed in the Temple. Several Psalms likewise reflect the
presence of the Tabernacle within the Temple precincts.[28] The
bicolon of Ps. 26:8 sets Temple and Tabernacle in parallel, thus:

yhwh 'hbty mʿwn bytk

[w]mqwm mškn kbwdk

YHWH I love the dwelling of your House, the place of
your glory's Tabernacle.[29]

---

[28] Virgil Rabe has discussed all of these examples in his study of *The Temple as
Tabernacle*, though in each pericope he has understood the parallels of Temple and
Tabernacle to be merely poetic images.

[29] Cf. Ps. 76:2f.

The similar expressions in the prose passages discussed above argue strongly against regarding the Tabernacle as merely a figurative parallel to the Temple here. In addition, the Tabernacle stands in another parallel position in Ps. 61:5 which, instead of pairing the Tabernacle with the Temple, pairs it with the shelter of YHWH's wings, thus:

'gwrh b'hlk ᶜwlmym

'ḥsh bstr knpyk

I shall dwell in your tent forever; I shall conceal myself in the covert of your wings.

That this refers to the wings of the cherubim has long been acknowledged.[30] Without denying the abstract nature of the image in this bicolon, one still must recognize that the source of the image of YHWH's tent in parallel with the "sēter of your wings" matches the arrangement of the Tabernacle under the wings of the cherubim as presented above.

The key terms ōhel, bêt YHWH, sēter, hêkāl, and sukkāh all cluster in Ps. 27:4f., thus:

אחת שאלתי מאת ה' אותה אבקש
שבתי בבית ה' כל ימי חיי
לחזות בנעם ה' ולבקר בהיכלו
כי יצפנני בסכה ביום רעה
יסתרני בסתר אהלו ...

I ask one thing of YHWH, that I shall
seek,
that I may dwell in the House of YHWH
all the days of my life
to envision the beauty of YHWH and to

---

[30] Rabe, *The Temple as Tabernacle*, p. 35; H. Kraus, *Psalmen* I (*Biblischer Kommentar Altes Testament* XV, 2nd ed., 1961) p. 433; A Weiser, *Die Psalmen, Das Alte Testament Deutsch* (Göttingen, Vandenhoeck and Ruprecht, 1959) 5th ed., p. 302; M. Dahood, *Psalms, The Anchor Bible* I, pp. 107f.; C.A. Briggs, *The Book of Psalms, ICC*, p. 66.

visit in his Temple
for he will conceal me in his pavilion
in a day of trouble,
he will hide me in the covert of his
tent. . .[31]

Parallels of "tent" and "tabernacle" (*'ōhel* and *miškān*) are common in Ugaritic as well (*UT*, 128:III:18-19; 2 *Aqht* V:31-3). These Biblical cases of parallel of tent terminology with that of the House of God, however, are more singular.

The parallel of Temple and Tabernacle appears once more in a Psalm mourning the destruction of the Temple, thus:

šlḥw b'š mqdšk
l'rṣ ḥllw mškn šmk

They case your Temple into the fire,
they profaned your name's Tabernacle
to the ground.

(Ps. 74:7)[32]

Reference to the destruction of the Tabernacle together with the Temple also occurs in the book of Lamentations, thus:

ויחמס כגן שכו שחת מעדו
שכח ה' בציון מועד ושבת
וינאץ בזעם אפו מלך וכהן
זנח אדני מזבחו נאר מקדשו
הסגיר ביד אויב חומת ארמנותיה
קול נתנו בבית ה' כיום מועד

And he has dealt violently with his
pavilion as with a garden,
he has destroyed his (Tent of) Meeting,
YHWH has caused holiday and Sabbath to
be forgotten in Zion,

---

[31] Cf. v. 6.

[32] Other Psalms which relate to Temple and Tabernacle are Pss. 15, 42, 43, 46, 76, 84.

> and he has spurned in his angry indigna-
> tion king and priest,
> the Lord has cast off his altar, abhorred
> his Temple,
> he has closed up the walls of her palaces
> in the hand of the enemy;
> they have made a noise in the House of
> YHWH as on a holiday.

(Lam. 2:6f.)

That $m^c d$ of the first bicolon refers to the 'ōhel mô'ēd in context seems clear. Against the objection that the Lamentations pericope may refer to the tent in a purely figurative sense, one must observe that the companion elements here are all real institutions—holiday, Sabbath, king, priest, altar, Temple—whose roles in Jerusalem were destroyed and are here bemoaned.

Josephus, too, states explicitly that the Tabernacle was brought into the Temple (*Jewish Antiquities*, VIII, 101; see also VIII, 106), though the usual cautions apply in weighing the testimony of late sources.

Rabbinic sources testify to the presence of the Tabernacle in the First Temple as well. The Rabbinic tradition that one of the five differences between the two Temples was that the šᵉkînāh dwelt in the First Temple but not in the Second may relate to the presence of the miškān only in the earlier building.[33] The cognates sᵉkînāh and miškān are certainly tied conceptually, the former denoting the divine presence and the latter denoting the medium of that presence.[34] The specific Talmudic assertion that the Tent of Meeting was stored away beneath the crypts of the (First) Temple is interesting to our study as well, though, again, one must exercise caution in view of the lateness of the statement.[35]

---

[33] *Babylonian Talmud*, Tractate *Yoma* 21b; cf. Rashi on Gen. 9:27.

[34] On the relationship of the terms škn, šᵉkînāh, and miškān, see Cross, "The Priestly Tabernacle," p. 227.

[35] *Babylonian Talmud*, Tractate *Ṣotah* 9a. It is possible that the Tabernacle was in fact stored in the manner which the Talmud states, while the appropriately measured space beneath the wings of the cherubim meanwhile corresponded to it above. Josephus in fact remarks that the effect of the spread-winged cherubim was precisely to appear as a tent (*Jewish Antiquities*, VIII, 103). This would still apply only to the First Temple, which alone would thus have housed both the actual Tabernacle and the cherubim.

The Deuteronomistic history, the Chronicler's history, Psalms, Lamentations, Josephus, and Rabbinic sources bear witness to the presence of the Tabernacle in the First Temple until the destruction. We now return to the Priestly writings themselves. The blessings of the Holiness Code culminate in a blessing which Cross has particularly emphasized as being crucial to the Priestly covenant theology.[36] Following a list of promises of agricultural and military security comes the simple, ultimate statement of YHWH's blessing:

> And I shall put my Tabernacle in your midst, and I myself shall not despise you. I shall walk about among you and shall become your God and you will become my people.

> (Lev. 26:11f.)

YHWH's presence among his people is, in the Priestly perspective, inextricably bound to the Tabernacle. The blessing here is simply and clearly that the Tabernacle will be present in Israel. The reference is not to the wilderness period, for every blessing preceding this one refers manifestly to the land. These verses must refer to a present, standing Tabernacle.[37] Scholars have, since Wellhausen, sought other institutions of which the Tabernacle is only a symbolic reflex owing to the fact that the original hypothesis viewed the post-destruction era as the proper locus of P. But nowhere in P is there the remotest hint that any other structure *can* fulfill the function of the Tabernacle. Nowhere in P is there a command concerning the disposition of the Tabernacle upon arrival in the land so as to create some link to a later institution. Priestly references to the *miqdāš* are unquestionably tied to the Tabernacle itself.[38] The *Tabernacle itself* is the pivotal concern of P. The institution of the priesthood, the first sacrifice in P, the first burning of incense—all occur together with the dedication of the Tabernacle. The command of Lev. 17 is unequivocal. One may not perform sacrifice anywhere but at *pétah 'ōhel mô͑ēd*; and this, P emphasizes repeatedly, is the law forever (*l͑lm*).[39] The implications of this fact for

---

[36] *CMHE*, p. 298.

[37] This recognition is presumably the reason for Engnell's having dated the Tabernacle traditions as pre-Jerusalemite.

[38] See for example Exod. 25:8f.

[39] Priestly references to laws which require the presence of the Tabernacle and

the dating of much of the Priestly material are crucial. Those accounts and legal materials in which the Tabernacle is vital and which insist on eternal centrality of that structure must be pre-Exilic. The alternative is to claim that the Priestly writers developed the theme of the Tabernacle as Israel's eternal channel to God shortly after the destruction of that channel. It is to picture an exiled Judean priest, in the years following the destruction of the centuries-old central national shrine, institutionalizing a programmatic doctrine that sacrifice must take place nowhere but at that shrine.[40] These Priestly materials are neither a program for, nor a reflection of, a restored Second Temple.

The matter of the ark, tablets, *urim* and *tummim*, and cherubim now becomes particularly significant. Whereas these Priestly concerns are particularly problematic for the models of Wellhausen and Kaufmann, as noted above, they now cease to be so. They belong exclusively to the First Temple. Their crucial place in the Priestly writings—tied inseparably to the Tabernacle—fortifies the notion that a large portion of P is a product of the First Temple era.

Further evidence points to the existence of much of the Priestly writing prior to the destruction. The tie between P and Ezekiel is patent and long-recognized. Their fund of shared terms is of course sizeable, suggesting that the two works are, at minimum, products of a common school.[41] Careful comparison indicates that their relationship is in fact even more direct and integral. Two portions of the book of Ezekiel are so clearly bound to corresponding Priestly pericopes as to require that we recognize the dependence of one upon the other.[42] The first such pairing is found in the visions of Ezekiel 5 and 6. YHWH's indictment of his people in Ezek. 5:7 asserts:

---

which are posed as eternal include Exod. 27:21; 28:43; 30:21; Lev. 3:17; 6:11; 10:9; 16:29, 34; 17:7; 24:3,8; Num. 18:23; 19:10.

[40] Ezekiel's prophecy that "my Tabernacle will be over you" (Ezek. 37:27) does not refer to rebuilding the Tabernacle, nor to cultic centralization. It clearly refers to the spreading of a heavenly tabernacle over the entire people of Israel.

[41] Cf. Driver, *ILOT*, pp. 139f., for a partial collection of P expressions of which many occur nowhere else but in the book of Ezekiel.

[42] The direction of dependence is discussed below. Cf. recent discussion and references in Haran, *Temples and Temple Service in Ancient Israel*. Haran argues forcefully for P's historical precedence to Ezekiel. See especially pp. 45-46, 72-76, 93-96, 102-111, 125-128, 187, 193-194, 225, 288,296-298.

bhqty l' hlktm w't mšpty l' ʿšytm

("You did not walk according to my statutes, and you did not do my judgments.") This is a variation of the positive and negative protases of the covenant blessings and curses of Leviticus 26. The blessings of the Priestly covenant are due *'m bhqty tlkw w't mṣwty tšmrw wʿšytm 'tm* ("If you walk according to my statutes and you keep my commandments and do them." Lev. 26:3). The curses are to fall . . . *'m bhqty tm'sw w'm 't mšpty tgʿl npškm lblty ʿšwt 't kl mṣwty* (". . .if you despise my statutes and disdain my judgments so as not to do all my commandments. . ." Lev. 26:15). Ezekiel's *rîb*[43] is thus grounded in the terms of the priestly covenant. The chastisement which YHWH tells Ezekiel is due includes the dreadful outcome that "fathers will eat sons in your midst, and sons will eat their fathers, and I shall do judgements in you, and I shall scatter your whole remnant to all the winds" (Ezek. 5:10). This chastisement itself echoes the covenant curses of Leviticus 26, which include the threat "you will eat the flesh of your sons. . ." (26:29). The term for *scattering* (Hebrew root: *zrh*) which occurs in the *rîb* of Ezekiel likewise appears in the curses of the Priestly covenant, Lev. 26:33; and Ezekiel's reference to a remnant (Hebrew root: *š'r*) recalls Lev. 26:36, 39. The tie of Ezekiel's *rîb* to Lev. 26 is particularly apparent in the language of Ezekiel 5:17.

> And I shall send hunger and evil beast over you, and they will bereave you, and pestilence and blood will pass through you; and I shall bring the sword over you. . .

Compare Lev. 26:22, 25.

> And I shall send the wild beast among you and it will bereave you. . . And I shall bring the sword over you. . . And I shall send pestilence in your midst. . .

The oracle which follows Ezek. 5:17 continues the judgment in the terms of the Priestly covenant, thus:

> . . . behold I am bringing the sword over you, and I shall destroy your high places, and your altars will be desolate

---

[43] I.e. a covenant litigation; Wright, "The Lawsuit of God. A Form Critical Study of Deut. 32," pp. 26-67.

and your images broken and I shall cast down your slain
before your idols. And I shall set the corpses of the
children of Israel before their idols, and I shall scatter
(*zrh*) your bones around your altars. In all your dwelling
places the cities will be wasted and the high places will
be desolate. . .

(Ezek. 6:3b-6a)

Compare Lev. 26:30, 31a.

And I shall destroy your high places and cut off your
idols, and I shall set your corpses on the corpses of your
idols. . . And I shall waste your cities and make your
sanctuaries desolate. . .

Ezekiel and P are not merely drawing on a common bank of
vocabulary. One depends directly on the other. A second example
of this dependence is found in Ezekiel 20. In this oracle of
Ezekiel, YHWH reviews the record of his people in the days of the
exodus, several times speaking in the very terms of Exodus 6 (P).
YHWH tells Moses: "I shall bring you to the land which I have
lifted up my hand to give to Abraham, Isaac, and Jacob, and I shall
give it to you. . ." (Exod. 6:8). YHWH tells Ezekiel: "I brought
them to the land which I lifted up my hand to give to them. . ."
(Ezek. 20:28; see also vv. 6,42). References to YHWH's making
himself known (*Niphal* of *yd'*) are also common to these two pericopes (Exod. 6:3; Ezek. 20:5) as are the references to YHWH's
outstretched arm (Exod. 6:6; Ezek. 20:33f.) and to the exodus itself
(Exod. 6:6f.; Ezek. 20:6,9). Echoes of Leviticus 26 may be heard
in this pericope of Ezekiel as well (Ezek. 20:8, compare Lev. 26:21;
Ezek. 20:13,16,24, compare Lev. 26:43). Again we are faced with a
case of direct dependence between Priestly materials and Ezekiel.

While the similarities between P and Ezekiel have often been
judged to be demonstrative that P is later than Ezekiel, analysis of
the pericopes which we have observed here suggests the opposite.
First, one would more naturally and properly expect to find a prophet quoting Torah than the reverse.[44] The retelling of the exodus
derives from the telling, and not the reverse. Proof that this is in
fact the way of things and not merely the imposition of our own
conceptual priorities lies in the observation that Ezekiel does

---

[44] Weinfeld makes this observation as well; cf. *DDS*, p. 183.

actually refer back to Torah (Ezek. 7:26; 22:26; see also 43:11; 44:5,23). A second indication that Ezekiel is not the influence behind P is that Ezekiel's conception of the Temple design goes quite unheeded in P. If P is prior, then this is no problem, because there is no reason why Ezekiel must necessarily model a Temple plan after the Priestly Tabernacle. If Ezekiel is prior, however, then where is his influence in this most central of all Priestly matters?[45] Surely in Ezekiel we see dependence upon P, and not the derivation of Priestly legislation and accounts from Ezekiel's visions.

We are drawn to a date for much of the Priestly writing which is pre-Exilic. Further considerations support this dating. The institution of the Autumnal New Year and Day of Atonement in P have long been taken to indicate a post-destruction dating because of their emphasis on guilt and repentance. The natural setting for national guilt seemed to be in the years when the prophets and leaders taught that the Exile was divine chastisement for national sin. One must ask, however, how such a law could possibly have been promulgated. If these two holidays were instituted as a direct response to the destruction and Exile, how could they possibly have been declared a short time later to have been written by Moses? The promulgation of new holidays and customs with a claim to antiquity can be successful at nearly any time *except* as response to a singular historical experience. New Year and Day of Atonement may well have been unknown through the time of the Josianic reform, as they are absent in JE and D. Their promulgation in the years following Josiah was certainly possible. One new Mosiac document had already been found, Passover had been renewed. Institution of new ceremonies was quite practicable politically. The feeling of guilt certainly was not absent either in the years following Josiah's reform, which had pronounced the centuries-old guilt of the nation and had predicted the imminence of the covenant curses. One can easily picture priests of that period establishing holidays of purported antiquity which offered atonement through repentance and sacrifice. After 587, however, such an action would have been all but impossible.

The institution of the New Year and Day of Atonement in P thus points to a pre-Exilic writing. At the same time it suggests the possibility of a post-Josianic writing. Numerous points of proximity

---

[45] On divergences between Ezekiel and P, see Kaufmann, *RI*, pp. 429, 432ff.

between P and Dtr[1] bolster this notion that much of P was composed close to the historical juncture of the Josianic reform, and prior to the destruction of Judah. Not the least of these is the matter of centralization. In focusing continually on the Tabernacle, P protests a bit too much for one to accept Wellhausen's claim that P *presumes* an accomplished centralization. On the contrary, the Priestly writer(s) seem to be fighting for the same objective as that of the Deuteronomists. This is not surprising given that both works stem from Priestly circles. It is difficult to separate the Deuteronomistic literature, including the book of Jeremiah, from the priestly circle of Anathoth,[46] while the P literature clearly attaches to the Aaronid priesthood. It is entirely appropriate that the literary activity of the Deuteronomists should have had a counterpart among the Aaronid priests. Certain similarities in the Deuteronomistic and Priestly centralization writings underscore this association of their interests. The Priestly centralization law of Leviticus 17, for example, concludes with the clause, "and they will no longer offer their sacrifices to the satyrs ($s^{ec}îrîm$) after which they whore..." (Lev. 17:7). The unusual reference to satyrs in this context becomes less enigmatic when one observes that the description of Josiah's centralization in 2 Kings 23 (Dtr[1]) particularly notes that Josiah "broke the *bāmôt* of the *satyrs*[47] which were at the gate of Joshua the officer of the city. . ." (2 Kings 23:8b). This mutual detail is accompanied by other points of association. In the previous chapter, Josiah's treatment of the priests of the *bāmôt* was discussed.[48] According to Dtr[1], "the priests of the *bāmôt* did not go up to the altar of YHWH at Jerusalem, but they did eat *maṣṣôt* among their brethren" (2 Kings 23:9). These priests were supported along with the Temple priests in Jerusalem, sharing in the holy victuals. They were, however, for some reason, not permitted to officiate in the priestly office at the altar. Interestingly, this is precisely the treatment of a blemished priest in the Holiness Code, thus:

> He shall eat the bread of his God, of the most holy and of the holy. But he shall not come to the *pārōket* and he

[46] See Cross, "The Priestly Houses of Early Israel," in *CMHE*, pp. 195-215: also Baruch Halpern, "Toward the Antecedents of Deuteronomy," Harvard Hebrew 200 paper (unpublished), 1974; Engnell, *A Rigid Scrutiny*, p. 62.

[47] The emendation of Noth (and others); see Noth, *Leviticus*, p. 131.

[48] See above, p.29.

shall not approach the altar, because he is blemished.

(Lev. 21:22f.)

The comparable treatment of the physically-blemished priest and the spiritually-blemished may well derive from the mutual concern of the priestly houses for the purity—and control—of the central altar.

The important Priestly provision for atonement in the event that the entire community of Israel sins through error likewise seems particularly relevant to the Josianic years. The pericope Lev. 4:13-21 poses a hypothetical case in which the entire nation transgresses any of the commandments of YHWH and later the transgression becomes known to them. Atonement for such a transgression is vested in the anointed priest at the Tent of Meeting. Again 2 Kings 22,23 comes to mind, in which Josiah rends his clothes upon hearing the words of the newly-discovered book and acknowledges YHWH's anger over Israel's not having observed the commands which are now made known. National sin owing to ignorance of YHWH's commands is precisely the platform on which the Josianic reform is predicated. The Priestly treatment of sacrifice to satyrs, disqualification of priests from attendance at the altar, and communal sin through ignorance—all attached integrally to passages which relate to the centralized service of the Tabernacle—point to composition in the same milieu as that of Dtr[1].

The association of P and Dtr[1] is apparent in several other points of similarity beyond the centralization issue as well. As discussed in the previous chapter,[49] one of the principal moments in the Deuteronomistic history is the portrayal of the events of the day in which the Temple of Solomon is dedicated. On that occasion, according to 1 Kings 8:10f., the glory and cloud of YHWH fill the Temple so that the priests are not able to stand and serve before it. The Priestly passage Exod. 40:34f. is unquestionably related to this Deuteronomistic one. The Priestly passage is part of the pericope in which the events of the day in which the Tabernacle is dedicated are portrayed. On that occasion, once, again, the glory

---

[49] See above, p. 38.

and cloud of YHWH fill the Tabernacle so that Moses is not able to enter.[50]

Another principal portrayal in the Deuteronomistic history, also discussed in the previous chapter,[51] is that of the confrontation of the prophet Elijah with the priests of Baʿl on Mount Carmel. There in response to Elijah's supplication at the altar:

> *Fire of YHWH fell and consumed the offering* and the wood and the stones and the dust and licked up the water which was in the trench; *and all the people saw, and they fell on their faces.* . .

(1 Kings 18:38f.)

This miraculous action is interpreted as divine confirmation of Elijah's position (v. 36). The Priestly portrayal of the inauguration of Aaron and his sons concludes with the same manner of divine confirmation following Aaron's first sacrifice:

> *Fire went out from before YHWH and consumed the offering* and the fat on the altar; *and all the people saw, and they shouted, and they fell on their faces.*

(Lev. 9:24)

The wording of the two passages is nearly identical and further fuels our perception of some association between the Deuteronomistic and Priestly literatures.[52] Several shared expressions in D and P verify this observation as well. The Deuteronomistic review of the wilderness episode of the spies includes Moses' reference to *tpkm 'šr 'mrtm lbz yhyh* ("your little ones whom you said would be a prey. . ." Deut. 1:39). This exact expression appears in the Priestly account of the incident (Num. 14:3,31). Carpenter and Harford-Battersby[53] and Driver[54] reckon these verses as J; but this results

---

[50] Weinfeld, *DDS*, p. 204, and Mendenhall, *The Tenth Generation*, p. 212, view the Exodus portrayal as deriving from that in 1 Kings. See also von Rad, "The Tent and the Ark," in *The Problem of the Hexateuch and Other Essays*, p. 118n.

[51] See above, pp. 64f.

[52] The nature of the association is discussed below.

[53] *The Hexateuch*, pp. 207, 209.

[54] *ILOT*, p. 62.

in breaking the continuity of both the J and P contexts, which otherwise separate and flow neatly through their respective portrayals of the episode.[55] Reckoning these verses as J, further, ignores the ironic sense of the P context, in which YHWH swears that "as you spoke in my hearing, so I shall do to you" (v. 28). The people had said that it would have been better to die in the desert than to fall by the sword in the new land, their children being taken as prey (vv. 2f.); and so YHWH declares that they will indeed die in the desert, but their children will arrive in the land which the parents have refused (vv. 29-33). The divisions of Carpenter and Harford-Battersby and of Driver split this context up the middle. Noth[56] and Kaufmann,[57] on the other hand, recognize these verses as Priestly. P and D thus share a specific expression in their respective portrayals of the spy incident. There may also be an association in the Priestly variations of the D reference to the condemnation of the "evil generation" in the spy episode (Deut. 1:35). The Priestly version, retaining its stock term for the nation, refers to the condemnation of the "evil congregation ($\bar{e}d\bar{a}h$)" (Num. 14:35). In a second reference to this event, P speaks of "the generation which did evil in the sight of YHWH" (Num. 32:13).

P and D also share certain terms in their portrayals of the exodus. Both use the rare $bhpzwn$ ("in haste"), though, interestingly, D utilizes the term to express the haste with which the Israelites leave Egypt, thus generating the custom of eating unleavened bread (Deut. 16:3), while P expresses therewith the haste with which the Israelites eat the paschal lamb (Exod. 12:11). D and P both refer to the "outstretched arm" of YHWH in their exodus portrayals as well (Deut. 7:19; 9:29; 11:2; 26:8; Exod. 6:6).

The numerous parallels between D and the Priestly Holiness code are well-known.[58] Here again a conceptual and terminological association between products of the Priestly and Deuteronomistic writers can hardly be denied.

---

[55] The Priestly text is Num. 13:1-17a,21,25f.,32f.; 14:1a,2f.,5-10,26-38. The J text is 13:17b-20,22-24,27-31; 14:1b,4,11-25,39-45.

[56] HPT, pp. 19, 123n.

[57] RI, pp. 439f.

[58] See Noth, Leviticus, p. 127; The Laws in the Pentateuch, pp. 8, 13, 23-26; Wellhausen, PHI, pp. 35n., 376ff. Cf. my discussion below.

The Priestly account of the rebellion of Korah likewise suggests the association of P and D; and, more important, it points to the nature of the association. While all of the primary sources of the Torah speak of the holiness of the entire people of Israel[59] the concept of ʿam⁻ qādōš is particularly emphasized in D. Its most significant consequence is the absence of the levels of holiness which characterize P. The fundamental distinction between the Priest and Levite with regard to territory (e.g. only an Aaronid priest may enter the Tabernacle) and responsibilities (e.g. only an Aaronid may approach the altar to offer sacrifice) which is clear in P is not delineated in D. The Korah account is apparently a Priestly response to the Deuteronomistic stance. Korah's claim against Moses and Aaron is that:

> You take too much, for all the congregation, all of them, are holy, and YHWH is in their midst; and why do you raise yourselves over the congregation of YHWH?

> (Num. 16:3)

Moses responds that YHWH will make known those whom he will bring near to himself as holy. The test is the offering of incense, a responsibility of the holy, and he adds a rebound of Korah's words: "*You* take too much, *Levites*" (v. 7). The outcome of the test is predictable. As YHWH rejects Korah's claim, P responds to the Deuteronomists.[60] The character of the Priestly narrative here marks it clearly as a composition designed as *response*. Whether that response is made to the Deuteronomistic (Anathoth, Mushite?) school in general or to the Torah book which they produced in particular remains to be seen.

We have seen thus far that significant portions of the Priestly Work were composed prior to the destruction and Exile and that these portions include both narrative and legal compositions, including parts of the Holiness Code and other legal units, as well as the large corpus of Tabernacle material. We have also seen that

---

[59] Exod. 19:6 (J); Lev. 19:2 (P); Deut. 7:6; 14:2,21; 26:19; 28:9.

[60] Cf. discussion of this narrative, particularly with regard to its relation to the Deuteronomistic literature and to Aaronid/Mushite polemic, in *CMHE*, pp. 205f.; Weinfeld, *DDS*, pp. 226-232; Paul Hanson, *The Dawn of Apocalyptic*, pp. 149n., 267ff.; von Rad, *Die Priesterschrift im Hexateuch*, pp. 109f.

much of this Priestly writing is related to the Deuteronomistic
Torah book and to the larger history of which it is a part, namely
Dtr[1]—at times pursuing the same interests as the Deuteronomistic
literature, at times engaging in polemic. That Priestly composition
should have occurred concurrently with Deuteronomistic composition is neither a surprising nor a new notion. Weinfeld has argued
for concurrent composition, though he understands the Deuteronomistic literature to derive from court scribal circles. He thus
explains the differences between the Deuteronomistic and Priestly
materials as the result of the distinct perspectives of the court and
the priesthood respectively.[61] The recent work concerning priestly
houses in Israel,[62] together with the clear association of the priests
Hilkiah and Jeremiah with the Josianic reform and the Deuteronomistic literature, suggest that Dtr[1] and P may derive rather from
the two priestly houses which are identified in recent scholarship as
Mushite and Aaronid. Thus the two works reflect a shared and crucial interest in the matter of centralization of worship while
reflecting very different ideas of the prerogatives of the priests and
Levites at the central place. Thus the works are of different styles
but occasionally share a term or phrase. Thus the works are essen-
tially independent, but matters which are related to key convoca-
tions in Dtr[1]—namely the Temple dedication, Elijah at Carmel, and
Josiah's reform—have reflexes in P. The Priestly treatment of the
New Year and Day of Atonement, of the matter of national sin
through ignorance and subsequent recognition, and of the questions
of holiness and Levitical prerogatives in the Korah pericope all suggest the likelihood that much of the Priestly work was composed in
response to the Josianic events and the Deuteronomistic literature.
This, again, is not terribly surprising. The royal and prophetic support of the promulgation of the book of the Torah lent prestige
and, more important, legitimacy to the faction which produced it.
Public reading gave it authority and fame. At the same time, however, the book of the Torah was anathema to the Aaronid priesthood. The book was tied to the JE sources, quoting them often on
matters which could not fail to offend the Aaronids, such as the
matter of the golden calf. Indeed, the only references to Aaron in
Deuteronomy, as has often been noted, are the two notices of his
death and his participation in the calf episode. The recurrences of

---

[61] Weinfeld, *DDS*, pp. 179-189.

[62] See above, n. 46.

this matter in Dtr[1] in association with the crime of Jeroboam I and its final cure in Josiah, who performs actions which are identical with those of Moses, were discussed in Chapter I.[63] The Dtr[1] portrayal of history could thus hardly have pleased the Aaronids. Composition of their own Torah documents, portraying the Mosaic age from their perspective, lending to their position the legitimacy which their rivals were achieving, was natural, advantageous, and perhaps critical. Composition of Priestly Torah was, further, not a new endeavor for this school; they certainly possessed documents which even pre-dated Deuteronomistic writings.[64] And now they had reason to produce more.

The presence of alternative *tôrôt* in the priestly houses of Judah between the time of Josiah and the Exile is witnessed in several passages in the books of Jeremiah and Ezekiel which have long been perplexing. In Jer. 8:8, the priest/prophet of Anathoth challenges the people thus:

> How do you say 'We are wise, and the Torah of YHWH
> is with us'? Behold it was made for a lie, the lying pen
> of scribes.

Jeremiah cannot possibly refer here to the Torah of the Deuteronomists. Its language pervades his own book, its conceptions are his own, it was promulgated by his friends and supporters,[65] and he lauds Josiah (Jer. 22:15f.). Further, Jeremiah is a staunch defender of the Torah, regularly attacking those who have forsaken it (Jer. 6:19; 9:12; 16:11; 26:4; 32:23). Scholars have nonetheless assumed that at that particular historical moment Jeremiah could only be refering to Deuteronomy.[66] Weinfeld has sought to soften the verse

---

[63] See above, pp. 8-9.

[64] See, e.g., W.L. Moran, "The Literary Connection between Lev. 11:13-19 and Deut. 14:12-28," *CBQ* 28 (1966), pp. 271-277, concerning the dependence of the Deuteronomic list of forbidden animals upon the Priestly version.

[65] See Halpern, "Toward the Antecedents of Deuteronomy," pp. 24ff.

[66] Cf. John Bright, *Jeremiah, the Anchor Bible*, p. 63; Kaufmann, *RI*, p. 421; Weinfeld, *DDS*, pp. 151n., 159n., 160; J.P. Hyatt, "Torah in the book of Jeremiah," *JBL* 60 (1941), pp. 383f. Hyatt regards the "Torah" here as referring to Deuteronomy, though he adds that it may here include other documents which those whom Jeremiah opposes regarded as Torah as well, including the Covenant Code and portions of H and P. He does not defend this speculation.

by understanding the word *šéqer* as meaning "in vain," rather than as "a lie." He notes the Greek Translation εἰς ματην in this regard. Bright and Hyatt have insisted upon the stronger translation.[67] But even if we follow Weinfeld's translation, the text is barely more favorable to the Torah and to those who produced it. Weinfeld has suggested that the sense of the verse is that Jeremiah is condemning the scribes "for not observing the teaching that they themselves had committed to writing: the pen of the scribes has composed to no purpose, the scribes have written in vain."[68] This reading, however, does not wholly convey the strength of the last words of the text: *ʿt šqr sprym*. It rather underscores the difficulty of reconciling these words to everything else which we know about Jeremiah's attitude toward the book. Jeremiah is rather attacking other, vain Torah.

Three pericopes in the book of Jeremiah point specifically to the author's acquaintance with portions of the Priestly literature. In the first (Jer. 4:19-27) Jeremiah again criticizes the people and again refers cynically to their supposed wisdom. In the midst of the oracle, he declares:

r'yty 't h'rṣ whnh thw wbhw w'l hšmym w'yn 'wrm

I looked at the earth and behold it was unformed and
void, and to the heavens and they had no light.

Without a doubt, this verse recalls the Priestly Creation account. More important, the sense of the verse is ironic and its context pejorative. In the Priestly account, the earth is unformed and void until Elohim forms seas and dry land. He then looks at the earth and sees that it is good (Gen. 1:10). Jeremiah reverses the process: YHWH looks a the earth, and it is unformed and void. In P there is darkness in the heavens until Elohim creates light. In Jeremiah, he looks and their light is gone.[69] Jeremiah knows this Priestly

---

[67] Hyatt, "Torah in the Book of Jeremiah," p. 382.

[68] *DDS*, p. 160. See also Weinfeld, "Jeremiah and the Spiritual Metamorphosis of Israel," *ZAW* 88 (1976), p. 28, where he notes that Hebrew *šqr* means "false," while *lšqr* means "in vain." Since both forms appear in this verse, the question of the meaning here remains open; and, to my mind, the force of the last three words, *ʿt šqr sprym*, is determinative.

[69] A.S. Kapelrud, "The Date of the Priestly Code," *ASTI* 3 (1964), pp. 58-64, has noted the use of the terms *thw wbhw* here in Jeremiah, but, failing to perceive the

account and reverses it in criticism of apparently the same parties whom he criticizes in Jer. 8:8.

A second reference to Priestly terminology appears in a Jeremianic pericope which particularly reflects the presence of the Deuteronomistic and Priestly alternative perspectives. As discussed above, the Priestly expression of the centralization of worship focuses on the Tabernacle and the ark while the Deuteronomistic expression is tied to the place (i.e. Jerusalem) where YHWH sets his name. In Jer. 3:16f., the prophet promises the transgressing Judeans that their repentance will bring blessing, so that:

> It will be, when you will multiply and be fruitful (*trbw wprytm*) in the land in those days, says YHWH, that they will no longer say, 'the ark of the covenant of YHWH' and it will not come to mind, and it will not be made anymore. At that time they will call Jerusalem the throne of YHWH and all the nations wil be gathered (*wnqww*) to it, to the name of YHWH, to Jerusalem. . . (MT)

At the same time that Jeremiah predicts the replacement of the concern for the ark by a concern for the place and the name, he promises the blessing which is a hallmark of P, "be fruitful and multiply,"[70] (again he reverses the order).[71] One should note also the use of the *Niphal wnqww* ("will be gathered"). The term is familiar from the Priestly Creation account, Gen. 1:9f.[72] These are the only two occurrences of the form in the Hebrew Bible. Again Jeremiah draws on the language of the other priestly house and its

---

relationship of the entire verse to Genesis 1, he has concluded that Jeremiah must have learned the expression from First Isaiah (Cf. Isa. 34:11, which in any event is probably not from the hand of First Isaiah) because Genesis 1, he assumes, must be Exilic.

[70] See Cross, *CMHE*, pp. 295., for discussion of this blessing, and references. See Weinfeld, "Jeremiah and the Spiritual Metamorphosis of Israel," pp. 19-26, for defense of the originality of this verse to Jeremiah. Weinfeld also points to the reflection in this verse of the opposing Deuteronomistic and Priestly viewpoints.

[71] See S. Talmon's discussion of stylistic metathesis and textual inversion in "The Textual Study of the Bible—A New Outlook," pp. 358-378.

[72] See also its reflex in the P blood plague account, Exod. 7:19, and discussion in Ziony Zevit, "The Priestly Redaction and Interpretation of the Plague Narrative in Exodus," *JQR* 66 (1976), p. 199.

74

literature in his prophecy of the ultimate victory of his own position.

Jeremiah's classic attack upon the efficacy of sacrifice without obedience seems to reflect the alternative Torah compositions of the Deuteronomists and the Aaronid priestly house as well. The critical interest of the Priestly literature in sacrifice is patent. Deuteronomy, on the other hand, contains no comparable detailed legislation on the particulars of sacrifice. The conclusion of the Priestly manual of offerings (Lev. 1-7) states:

> This is the Torah of offering, grain offering, sin offering, trespass offering, installation offerings, sacrifice, and peace offerings which YHWH commanded Moses in Mount Sinai in the day that he commanded the Israelites to offer their sacrifices to YHWH in the wilderness of Sinai.

> (Lev. 7:37f.)

Jeremiah directly attacks this statement, thus:

> For I did not speak with your fathers and I did not command them in the day that I brought them out of the land of Egypt about matters of offering and sacrifice. But rather I commanded them this thing, saying: Listen to my voice, and I shall be your God and you will be my people; and you shall walk in all the way which I shall command you, so that it will be good for you.

> (Jer. 7:22f.)

Jeremiah's reference to the day that YHWH brought Israel out of Egypt applies to the entire wilderness period, as is evidenced by the wording of the next verse, which quotes directly from the language of Deuteronomy (i.e. from the Plains of Moab at the end of the forty years in the wilderness).[73] He challenges here the specific claim of the Aaronids that their Torah of offerings was divinely ordained in the wilderness.[74] One should take special note of the

---

[73] On the Deuteronomistic interest in Egypt, see the discussion in Chapter I, pp. 31-32.

[74] See Weinfeld's treatment of this pericope; "Jeremiah and the Spiritual Metamorphosis of Israel," pp. 52-55, defending Jeremiah's authorship (though he sees "Deuteronomic adaptation" in v. 23). Weinfeld observes that this statement of Jeremiah

alternative which Jeremiah juxtaposes to the challenge. It is specifically the wording of Deuteronomy which Jeremiah opposes to the sacrificial laws of P. When he quotes YHWH as having commanded Israel to "listen to my voice," he is using precisely the command which introduces the blessings (Deut. 28:1) and the curses (28:15) of the Deuteronomic covenant. The promise "so that it will be good for you" is likewise a common Deuteronomic component,[75] and the entire expression "you shall walk in all the way which I shall command you, so that it will be good for you" appears in Deut. 5:30. The language of these pericopes from the book of Jeremiah argues most strongly that the priestly houses of Judah were each engaged in the composition of Torah literature and that the writings of each received a less-than-cordial welcome from the other.

At nearly the same time that Jeremiah attacks those who ignore the Deuteronomic Torah, Ezekiel attacks priests who have done violence to the Priestly Torah and have ignored its precepts. According to Ezek. 22:26,

> Her priests have done violence to my Torah and have profaned my holy things; they have not distinguished between holy and profane, and they have not made known (the difference) between unclean and clean. . .[76]

This accusation is based upon the direct charge of YHWH to Aaron in Lev. 10:10.

> To distinguish between the holy and the profane, and between the unclean and the clean.

Not to overstate the case, one must certainly recognize the presence of common concerns of Jeremiah and Ezekiel and of the priestly houses from which they come. Both Jeremiah and Ezekiel attack priests, prophets, kings, and the nation for violating fundamental commands. At the same time, though, it seems impossible to deny the presence of a tension which their perspectives and their language reflect. They are both products of an age in which two

is "a slap in the face for the Priestly Code. . ."

[75] Deut. 4:40; 5:16,26; 6:3,18; 12:25,28; 22:7.

[76] Cf. Zeph. 3:4.

priestly houses were close to power and in which each sought to enhance its claim to legitimacy by making an appeal to ancient traditions which bore the authority of Israel's ideal age.[77]

The conclusion seems inescapable that a large portion of P is a product of the age preceding Exile, composed for many of the same objectives as the Deuteronomistic literature, and combining old and new writings as does the Deuteronomistic literature.[78] At the same time this is not to deny that significant portions of P are Exilic (discussed below) and that the final creation of the unified Priestly Work was Exilic or post-Exilic. The next task at hand, therefore, is quite the same as the task of Chapter I, namely to separate the pre-Exilic from the Exilic material and to examine the impact of the Exilic redaction upon the final product. This will also return us to the question which Cross, Engnell, and Noth have discussed as to whether P existed at any stage as an independent source.

We have already observed that D reflects a familiarity with the old sources JE, quoting them,[79] presuming the reader's acquaintance with them,[80] building upon them.[81] If D was

[77] The changes of kings and priests in the years following Josiah may provide the historical/political setting for the conflict of priestly houses and for the promulgation of each Torah. See the letter of Shemaiah the Nehelamite, Jer. 29:24-29 (as quoted by Jeremiah) from Babylon to Jerusalem addressed to Zephaniah ben Maaseiah the priest, saying: "YHWH has set you as priest in place of Jehoiada the priest. . ." and instructing Zephaniah to rebuke Jeremiah. Zephaniah is the name of the kōhēn mišneh whom Nebuchadnezzar executes (2 Kings 25:18-21; Jer. 52:24-27).

[78] As my interest is primarily literary, I have not introduced linguistic analysis into the body of the present discussion of the pre-Exilic origin of much of P. Recent studies which provide strong support of this dating on linguistic grounds are Avi Hurvitz, "The Evidence of Language in Dating the Priestly Code," *RB* 81 (1974), pp. 24-56; Jacob Milgrom, *Studies in Levitical Terminology*, I; Milgrom, *Cult and Conscience*, especially pp. 121ff. The work of Robert Polzin, *Late Biblical Hebrew: Toward an Historical Typology of Biblical Hebrew Prose*, also establishes the closeness of his Pg to Classical Biblical Hebrew (represented by JE, the Court History of David, and Dtr; Polzin's Dtr corresponds to my Dtr¹), sharing twice as many linguistic features with Classical BH as with the Late Biblical Hebrew of his Ps and the Chronicler. While I differ with Polzin on several assignments of individual verses to Pg or Ps, his Pg corresponds on the whole to those Priestly texts which I identify as pre-Exilic; see below.

[79] E.g., Deut. 7:20; cf. Exod. 23:28. Deut. 9:6,13; cf. Exod. 32:9; 33:3,5; 34:9. Deut. 9:9; cf. Exod. 34:28. Deut. 10:1; cf. Exod. 34:1. Deut. 11:6; cf. Num. 16:30,32a.

[80] E.g., Deut. 24:9; cf. Num. 12:1ff.

unsatisfactory to the Aaronids, JE must have been even more so. The JE treatment of the golden calf episode details Aaron's role more than in the book of Deuteronomy, while merit is ascribed to the zealous Levites. Aaron and Miriam are reprimanded for criticizing Moses.[82] Laymen perform sacrifices and enter the Tabernacle. Moses is clearly the dominant figure over Aaron. These specific features of JE were certainly unwelcome, if not properly offensive, to the Aaronids. In P YHWH communicates regularly with both Aaron and Moses. In P there is not a single sacrifice prior to the erection of the Tabernacle and the consecration of the priesthood (Exodus 40). Only a priest may perform a sacrifice, and in only one place. In the priestly portrayal of history there is never an appearance of an angel. There is never an account of a dream. There is never a portrayal of YHWH so anthropomorphic as the JE portrayals of YHWH's walking in the garden, standing on a rock in the wilderness, wrestling with Jacob, making Adam's and Eve's loincloths, and closing Noah's ark. The Priestly writers were acquainted with the JE sources and followed their narrative sequence, as Mowinckel has demonstrated,[83] but the priests retold that story in a manner which did not offend their own sensitivities. In short, the Priestly Torah compositions are as much an alternative to JE as they are to D.

This provides us with an important key to separating the several hands within P. Cross has described the activity of a Priestly tradent in Exile, who constructed the Priestly work out of several discrete documents which were at his disposal—including JE, the Covenant Code, and writings of his own Priestly forebears—and also expanded on the received texts himself. This Exilic tradent utilized two documents for the construction of a framework for his sources and compositions. These were the *tôlᵉdōt* book and the list of the Wilderness Stations of Israel's journeys (Numbers 33). The Exilic tradent's task was manifestly not the composition of alternative Torah to JE and D, but just the opposite: to house the various conflicting materials within the *tôlᵉdōt* and Stations framework so as to achieve a single, unified Torah. Thus the tradent set ten *tôlᵉdōt* headings[84] and twelve Station headings[85]

---

[81] E.g., Deuteronomy 31; see Chapter I, pp. 13ff.

[82] See Cross's treatment of these wilderness rebellion accounts in the context of the relationship of the priestly houses, *CMHE*, pp. 198-200, 203f.

[83] See above, n. 8.

[84] Gen. 2:4a; 5:1; 6:9; 10:1; 11:10,27; 25:12,19; 36:1; 37:2.

78

upon sections of his work, some of these sections containing mixtures of JE and P.[86] One must therefore differentiate between the hand of the unifying Exilic tradent and the pre-Exilic hand(s) which composed those portions of P which are alternative to parallel passages in JE and Dtr[1]. What would be the point, for example, of composing Priestly accounts which systematically avoid portraying any sacrifice by anyone prior to the consecration of Aaron and the Tabernacle if these accounts are being composed for a work which combines them with JE (which includes numerous sacrifices by Noah and the patriarchs)? The Priestly retelling of JE tales, removing all appearances of angels and dreams, seems likewise an impossible enterprise for the tradent who is combining the Priestly products with the very JE versions which they retell. The systematic Priestly presentation of the Metamorphosis of revelation of the divine name (*Elohim* to Noah, *El Shadday* to the patriarchs, *YHWH* to Moses), as well, must be the product of those priestly writers who composed alternative literature to JE, for this entire enterprise—which after all was the first key to the multiplicity of Pentateuchal sources[87]— is pointless for the tradent who is elaborating upon J. It is possible to conceive of historical circumstances in which the Exilic tradent was willing—or bound—to combine conflicting traditions, as will be discussed below. It is quite another thing, however, to picture that tradent himself composing the conflicting materials as elaboration of the received texts which they contradict. One may caution us here against imposing our own post-Hellenic conceptions of what is contradictory upon the minds of priests of the Sixth Century B.C. We shall see below, however, examples of the Priestly tradent's own conscious attempts to reconcile contradictions between received texts which clearly troubled him.

Textual evidence confirms this conceptual distinction between the two principal stages of the Priestly work. There are six cases of doublets between the tradent's frameworks and Priestly material which they enclose. (1) The *tôlᵉdōt* list reports the progeny of Noah in Gen. 5:32b, "And Noah begat Shem, Ham, and Japheth."

---

[85] Exod. 12:37a; 13:20; 14:1f; 15:22a; 16:1; 17:1a; 19:2; Num. 10:12; Num. 20:1a,22; 21:10f.; 22:1.

[86] Cross, *CMHE*, p. 304.

[87] Even prior to Jean Astruc the medieval Rabbinic commentators confronted this problem.

The Priestly Flood account, which commences in the following chapter, informs us anew that "Noah begat three sons, Shem, Ham, and Japheth" (6:10). This is not an epanalepsis enclosing the intervening J narrative (6:1-8), for the verse which precedes the doublet (6:9) is P and clearly has the character of an introduction of a new account. The hand which constructed the *tôl°dōt* framework, therefore, was not the hand which composed the Priestly Flood account. This is further confirmed by the fact that, when the J and P Flood accounts are separated, each flows neatly. The P account thus was originally a separate composition and was secondarily combined with the J account under the *tôl°dōt* heading, rather than being elaborative material which the Exilic tradent composed as part of his unified work.

(2) The *tôl°dōt* list reports the age of Noah (six hundred years) at the onset of the Flood (7:6). The same statistic appears in the Priestly account (7:11). That 7:6 indeed derives from the *tôl°dōt* list is clear in that it is the necessary connector between 5:32 and 9:28.

3) The *tôl°dōt* list reports the progeny of Shem, Gen. 11:10f. This is also reported in 10:22,31 (P).

(4) The *tôl°dōt* list then continues to the report that Terah begat Abraham, Nahor, and Haran (11:26). The Priestly tradent then introduces the Abrahamic materials with his adopted formula: "These are the *tôl°dōt* (of) Terah" (v. 27a).[88] The Priestly remark which follows is a doublet of the *tôl°dōt* report, thus: "Terah begat Abraham, Nahor, and Haran." Again, the hand which modeled the framework upon the *tôl°dōt* list was not the hand which wrote this P passage.

(5) The *tôl°dōt* (of) Esau are particularly interesting in this regard, because here we have a case of a contradicting doublet. The names of the wives of Esau in the list of Genesis 36 do not match those in Gen. 26:34; 28:9 (P). In Gen 36:2f. Esau married Adah the daughter of Elon the Hittite, Aholibamah the daughter of Anah the daughter of Zibeon the Hittite, and Basemath the the daughter of Ishmael and sister of Nebaioth. In Gen. 26:34; 28:9, Esau marries Judith the daughter of Beeri the Hittite, Basemath the daughter of Elon the Hittite, and Mahalath the daughter of Ishamel and sister of Nebaioth.[89] The relationship of the two texts is

---

[88]Cross. *CMHE*, p. 303.
[89]LXX the same.

obviously complex, neither depending directly upon the other. Neither then is the work of a tradent who depends upon the other as his source.

(6) The seventh Station notice of the Exilic tradent reports, "And they journeyed from Rephidim and came to the wilderness of Sinai and encamped in the wilderness" (Ex. 19:2). The tradent drew this report from the List of Stations (Num. 33:15). It is a clear doublet of the P verse which precedes it (19:1) and which has already reported their arrival in Sinai, thus: "In the third month after the exodus of the children of Israel from the land of Egypt, in that day they came to the wilderness of Sinai." In this case, as in the *tôl°dōt* doublets, the narrator and the editing tradent are two personages, each contributing to a separate stage of the Priestly work.

It should be noted here that this separation of the tradent's framework from portions of the Priestly account sheds light on the question of whether P ever existed as an independent source. While Cross and Engnell have argued that P did not exist independently, Noth has remarked, as quoted above,[90] that the P elements connect smoothly with each other, thus suggesting a once-independent, complete corpus. If, however, we separate out the *tôl°dōt* and Station headings, which are part of the second, combinatory stage of JEP, the Priestly material which remains does not "connect smoothly" at several junctures. This absence of a flowing P text, together with the omissions which Cross has noted in P (discussed above), suggests that the pre-Exilic Priestly literature was a collection of literary compositions which were perhaps not organized and united until their integration, along with JE, into the complete Priestly work in Exile.

In order to say anything more about the character of Priestly composition at each of its stages, we first must analyze each Priestly pericope in the Pentateuch and determine whether it is alternative literature to JE and D, or if it is to be reckoned to the organizing and elaborating hand of the Priestly tradent in Exile.[91] At the same time this will afford us insight into the character of the literary

---

[90] See above, n. 6.

[91] In the course of this analysis I refer to the person responsible for the redaction of the Priestly work as the Priestly tradent, following Cross. As in my treatment in Chapter I of those responsible for producing Dtr[1] and Dtr[2], I intend by the term *tradent* one whose task includes both editing and composition.

enterprise at each stage of the Priestly work.[92]

The Creation, Gen. 1:1-2:3. This text is already widely recognized as pre-dating the Exile, or at minimum as based upon such a text.[93] The precise form in which it now appears may owe in some degree to the Exilic tradent's remodeling, but the number of doublets as well as differences between it and the J version of Creation which follows—which are familiar—still points to the original independence of its core. Further, the structure of the cosmos which the Priestly Creation account portrays—a cosmic bubble of sky over earth with water above and below—is fundamental to the Priestly Flood account which follows.[94] Since, as discussed above, the Flood account is alternative rather than elaborative, and therefore prior to the Exilic tradent, the Creation account on which it depends must of course also be prior to that tradent. The reference to the P account in Jer. 4:22f., discussed above, further substantiates this dating.

"These are the *tôlᵉdōt* (of) heaven and earth when they were created," Gen. 2:4a. This Priestly heading to the J account of Creatrion, Eden, and the fraticide is part of the Exilic tradent's framework of ten unifying headings drawn from or imitative of the *tôlᵉdōt* book. That it is a heading and not a conclusion (nor a relocated statement which originally preceded Gen. 1:1) has been argued by Cross.[95]

tôlᵉdōt 'ādām, Gen. 5:1-28,30-32. This is the Exilic tradent's

---

[92] A verse summary of the texts of each stage appears in the Appendix.

[93] Noth, *HPT*, pp. 10f.; Cross, *CMHE*, p. 301, 305; John Kselman, "The Poetic Background of Certain Priestly Traditions," (Harvard Dissertation, 1971); von Rad, *Genesis*, pp. 61f.; E.A. Speiser, *Genesis, The Anchor Bible*, pp. 10f.

[94] In the Priestly account, the fountains of the deep are divided, thus causing the waters to flow up from below; and the windows of heaven are divided, thus causing the waters to flow down from above. The P flood is thus a cosmic crisis in which the habitable "bubble" is threatened. In the J version it simply rains.

[95] *CMHE*, p. 302; as opposed to Noth, *HPT*, p. 17, n. 41; Carpenter and Harford-Battersby, *The Hexateuch*, p. 1n.; von Rad, *Genesis*, p. 61; Driver, *ILOT*, p. 6n.

first use of the actual *tôlᵉdōt* book, whose structure ("PN lived x years and begat PN', and PN lived y years after begetting PN' and begat sons and daughters, and all the days of PN were z (x + y) years, and he died.") differs from the tradent's imitations of it. It is thus an older Priestly source which the Exilic tradent expanded into a framing device.

The Flood, Gen. 6:9-22; 7:11,13-16a,24; 8:1,2a,3b,4,5,7,-13a,14-19; 9:1-17. As we have already observed, the Priestly Flood account, when separated from the J account, is complete and fluent. As Mowinckel has pointed out, it follows the J account with regard to plot and order of details.[96] Its differences are nonetheless obvious and significant. Especially noteworthy is the portrayal of the number of animals in each version. In J, Noah takes seven pairs of clean animals and one pair of unclean animals into the ark. In P he takes only one pair of each, with no reference to the clean/unclean distinction. This is part and parcel of P's consistent presentation in which there can be no sanctioned sacrifice prior to the consecration of Aaron and the Tabernacle. In J, Noah's first act upon leaving the ark is to construct an altar and offer some of each species of clean animals as sacrifices, the aroma of which pleases YHWH (8:20f.), hence the need to portray Noah as having brought more than a single pair of these species into the ark. Were Noah to have carried only one pair, his sacrifice would have wiped out an entire species! In the Priestly conception, the righteous Noah cannot possibly perform a sacrifice and therefore requires no extra sacrificeable animals. The Priestly Flood account is thus not the Exilic tradent's expansion of the J text, but a complete and independent composition of an earlier Priestly writer, retelling the old JE tale from the Priestly perspective. Its original independence from the JE version is further substantiated by the presence of doublets. Thus the notation that Noah and his family entered the ark (7:13) is a Priestly repetition of the same notation in J (7:7). Other doublets include the statement *wygbrw hmym,* "And the waters prevailed," in Gen. 7:18 (J) and 7:24 (P); and the statement that the waters gradually receded, expressed as *hlwk wšwb* in 8:3a (J) and as *hlwk wḥswr* in 8:5a (P). Alternative to J, secondarily combined with it, the Priestly Flood account was an old composition which the Exilic tradent used.

---

[96] Mowinckel, *Erwägungen zur Pentateuch Quellenfrage,* pp. 28f.

The years of Noah, Gen. 7:6; 9:28f. These notices derive from the *tôlᵉdōt* book. The references to the Flood as a temporal point of reference, though differing from the usual pattern of the list, are quite as appropriate here as in the Shem genealogy (11:10).

The *tôlᵉdōt* (of) the sons of Noah, Gen. 10:1-7,20,22,23,-31,32. As is clear from the absence of the standard *tôlᵉdōt* pattern, this Priestly genealogy does not derive from the *tôlᵉdōt* book. Indeed, as discussed above, this genealogy includes in vv. 22,31 a doublet of the *tôlᵉdōt* book's Shem genealogy. Neither list, therefore, is a composition of the Exilic tradent. Both, rather, are older documents which that tradent handled. The initial words (10:1a) are the Exilic tradent's heading.

The *tôlᵉdōt* (of) Shem, Gen. 11:10-26,32. This is the continuation of the *tôlᵉdōt* book from 9:29. The initial words, "These are the *tôlᵉdōt* (of) Shem," are the Exilic tradent's heading.

The migration of Terah and Abraham, Gen. 11:27,31; 12:4b,5. Again the initial words "These are the *tôlᵉdōt* (of) Terah," are probably the Exilic tradent's unifying addition. The text, separated from the adjacent J material, flows neatly through the destruction of the cities of the plain.[97] It seems to be alternative rather than elaborative of the J text. The J account does not include the intermediate stop in Haran. The insertion of the Priestly notice of this stop in the midst of the J account does not enhance the text but rather creates confusion, for in the combined product YHWH now tells Abram *in Haran* to leave his land and his birthplace—but his land and birthplace are in Ur of the Chaldees. To appreciate the contradiction which this combination of J and P creates, one need only observe the extremes to which the Medieval commentators went in debating the solution to the problem.[98] Modern critics have suggested that the reference to Ur of the Chaldees is a reconciling gloss.[99] They note that later in J Abraham's family is at Haran, not Ur (29:4). But one must ask what the advantage of such a gloss would possibly be. It in no way makes the text any more sensible than it would have been without

---

[97] See next heading.

[98] See Rashi on Gen. 12:1; Ramban on Gen. 11:28; 12:1, and his references to Ibn Ezra. Even if we translate Hebrew *mwldt* more broadly than meaning strictly "birthplace," the text is awkward, as Medieval and modern commentators have sensed.

[99] Carpenter and Harford-Battersby, *The Hexateuch*, p. 18; von Rad, *Genesis*, p. 154.

it. The critics would have done better to suggest that "Ur of the Chaldees" was not merely a gloss but a replacement of the word "Haran" which originally stood in that context. But even on this solution, one must then claim that the J reference to Ur of the Chaldees in Gen. 15:7 is also a change. But the change in Gen. 15:7 is quite unnecessary, since either Haran or Ur would have made sense in that context. Obviously the problem is complex, but in no solution is it possible for the Priestly material to be an expansion of the J text. One must conclude that the Priestly migration notice is to be numbered among the Priestly compositions which, written as alternative to JE and D, preceded the Exilic tradent. The doublet of Lot's making the journey with Abram (cf. J v. 4a, and P v. 5a) further confirms this conclusion.

Lot, Gen. 13:6,11b,12a; 19:29. As observed above, the P Lot notices, when separated from their J environment, flow comfortably from the migration notices, so that P appears here to be a summary version of the extended J account. The reason for the brevity of P here becomes quite clear when one recalls the total absence of angelic creatures on earth in all Priestly materials. The J version of the destruction (Genesis 19), in which the two angels are catalysts of the action, was most certainly unsatisfactory to the Priestly writer. Again the Priestly notices can hardly be elaborative, first because they add nothing substantive to the JE narrative, and second because elaboration does not solve the problem of dealing with the unsatisfactory J angelic element. The hand which assembled the Priestly work did not compose the Lot notices, but rather inherited them.

Hagar and Ishmael, Gen. 16:1a,3:15,16. The same observations apply here as to the Lot pericope. The summary Priestly verses regarding Hagar and the birth of Ishmael, when separated from their J environment, are complete and flow satisfactorily. They add nothing but dates to the JE account. There is a contradiction between J and P regarding who is to name the child (cf. J, v. 11, and P, v. 15). And P has once again managed to tell the story without referring to the angel who is meanwhile crucial to the JE version. Again we have a text which the Exilic tradent received and combined, somewhat uncomfortably, with another received text.

The Abrahamic covenant, Genesis 17. P continues to retell major elements of the JE narrative, and, in the portrayal of the Abrahamic covenant, leaves the summary style of the preceding P sections and properly develops a theme for the first time since the portrayal of the Flood and Noahic covenant. Though its author was clearly familiar with JE tradition, the Priestly version of the Abrahamic covenant is nonetheless an originally independent composition, secondarily integrated into the Priestly work along with the JE version (Genesis 15). The following facts require this conclusion: (1) Up to this point in the Priestly materials, God has not communicated with Abraham. Whereas in J Abraham's migration follows a divine command, in P the motivation is not portrayed. Gen. 17:1 opens the account with God's self-introduction to Abraham (as *'ēl šadday*), an opening which is manifestly appropriate provided that the preceding JE material is *not* presumed. That this is a self-introduction based on new acquaintance and not the formal covenant element of introduction of the superior of the covenanting parties[100] is clear from the corresponding Priestly portrayal of God's self-introduction to Moses (as YHWH) in a non-covenantal meeting (Exod. 6:2f.). (2) While the J version of the Abrahamic covenant includes a portrayal of the ceremony of Abraham's performing covenant sacrifices and dividing the animals in halves, the Priestly version has no such ceremony. This is not because P depends and elaborates upon the J ceremony, for the two are separated in the Priestly work by chronological notices which mark the passage of thirteen years (Gen. 16:16; 17:1a). The absence of the covenant sacrifice in P rather is consistent with the total absence of sacrifice by any character in P prior to the consecration of the Tabernacle. Not even figures of the stature of Noah and Abraham may perform a sacrificial rite. The removal of this element which so dominates the J version of the Abrahamic covenant makes no sense if Genesis 17 is the work of the Priestly tradent in Exile who assembled the Priestly work. It must be one of that tradent's received texts. (3) The naming of Isaac in Genesis 17 is a contradicting doublet with the portrayal of that naming in Genesis 18 (J). In the Priestly portrayal it is Abraham who laughs, and hence the etiology of the name (17:17). In J it is Sarah (18:12). (4) The naming of Isaac in J comes in a pericope involving the visit of angels to Abraham and Sarah. As we have seen, all such portrayals in JE and D are eliminated in P. The Priestly version of the Abrahamic covenant must, therefore, have been composed independently of the JE narratives of Genesis 15 and 18, prior to the Exilic tradent.

---

[100] See Mendenhall, *Law and Covenant in Israel and the Ancient Near East,* Baltzer, *The Covenant Formulary,* p. 11.

The birth of Isaac, Gen. 21:1b,2b-5. This pericope conceivably is the elaboration of the Exilic tradent upon the J and E reports which it adjoins. The integral tie of its data with the Abrahamic covenant prediction, however, suggests that the two were once a single account which was divided and redistributed by the Exilic tradent. When joined, the two pericopes flow comfortably. The rather clumsy repetition of the datum in vv. 1a (J) and 1b (P) further casts doubt on the likelihood that this material is elaborative.

The purchase of Machpelah, Genesis 23. The account of Abraham's purchase of the cave and field of Machpelah is one of the few instances of Priestly composition in Genesis which may properly be termed narrative, as opposed to the usual succinct reports of events.[101] It is a unique unit, neither elaborating a JE narrative nor alternative to one.[102] In light of this unique character, Cross reckons Genesis 23 as a discrete document which the Priestly tradent in Exile used as a supplement to his other sources.[103]

The death of Abraham, Gen. 25:7-11a. This passage is not alternative to any JE materials. Its "And these are. . ." opening is common in the Priestly tradent's framework headings ("And these are the names. . .;" "And these are the *tôlᵉdōt*. . ."). It is probably the tradent's elaboration of shorter notices of the years and death of Abraham in J, P, or perhaps the *tôlᵉdōt* book.

The *tôlᵉdōt* (of) Ishmael, Gen. 25:12-17. The hand of the Exilic tradent is apparent here, attaching the *tôlᵉdōt* rubric (v. 12) to the received genealogical document.

The *tôlᵉdōt* (of) Isaac, Gen. 25:19f. The *tôlᵉdōt* heading of v. 19 is the tradent's introduction of the stories of Jacob and Esau which occur during the lifetime of Isaac. The notice of the marriage of Isaac and Rebekah which follows (v. 20) seems to introduce Rebekah as if the entire narrative of Genesis 24 were not present. This verse is therefore more probably a portion of one of the Exilic tradent's received texts than a part of his own construction. The long version of the mission of Abraham's servant to find a wife for Isaac may have been unsatisfactory to the Priestly writers

---

[101] Cf. Mowinckel, *Erwägungen zur Pentateuch Quellenfrage*, p. 30.

[102] Its style is sufficiently different from other P materials to have led Speiser to assign it, mistakenly, to J; *Genesis*, p. 173.

[103] *CMHE*, p. 305.

on any of several grounds, not the least of which is the presence of two references to YHWH's angel (24:7,40).

The wives of Esau, Gen. 26:34f. We have already noted the presence of a conflicting doublet between this account and the *tôlᵉdōt* enumeration of the names of the wives of Esau (Genesis 36). This account, further, must have been composed as alternative to the JE version. The Priestly writer here is certainly familiar with the JE tradition that, owing primarily to the initiative of Rebekah, Jacob travels to her brother Laban and marries his daughters. In the Priestly version, however, this acquisition of wives becomes the motive of Jacob's travels rather than a side effect. The JE portrayal of the conflict between Jacob and Esau over birthright and blessing is jettisoned. Interesting parallels of language remain. In the J account, for example, the twins struggle in Rebekah's womb, prompting her to exclaim, "If it is thus, *lmh zh 'nky*." In the Priestly version, it is Esau's Hittite wives which agitate Rebekah, and she exclaims that if Jacob takes Hittite wives as well, "*lmh ly ḥyym.*"[104] This Priestly material was apparently composed with the author's knowledge of the JE account, yet the Priestly author remodeled and shortened the story, eliminating its anecdotal character. This is again a case of alternative, rather than elaborative, composition.

Jacob in Paddan-Aram, Gen. 31:18b; 33:18b. If any Priestly account of Jacob's years in Paddan-Aram ever did exist, we apparently do not have it in the Priestly work. The two short Priestly comments seem to be rather the elaborative remarks of the tradent who assembled the Priestly work. The first, 31:18b, merely notes Jacob's acquisition of material goods in Paddan-Aram. The second, 33:18b, is clearly an editorial solution to one of the problems of combination of sources. The JE material which precedes this comment concludes with Jacob's arrival at Shechem. The next Priestly material, however, speaks of an appearance of God to Jacob "when he was coming from Paddan-Aram" (35:9) at Bethel. Since the author of this Priestly Bethel account apparently produced no prior Shechem account, it was perfectly appropriate to speak of the events at Bethel as taking place "when he was coming from Paddan-Aram." The Exilic tradent's combination of this material

---

[104] The Priestly reference to Jacob's leaving "*bbrkw 'tw*" ("when he blessed him") may also pun, conssciously or unconciously, on the E reference to Jacob's leaving "*bbrḥw*" ("when he fled").

88

with the JE Shechem account, however, rendered this wording somewhat awkward, i.e. it was strange to speak of Jacob as still on a journey from the East when he had already made a stay in the land. The tradent eased this awkwardness with the editorial comment of 33:18b, characterizing the Shechem stay as a station on the journey.

Jacob named Israel at Bethel, Gen. 35:9-15. That the author of this pericope was acquainted with the JE traditions of both Bethel and Penuel is obvious. At the same time, the very fact that he has combined the two tradition—i.e. the revelation and erection of a pillar at Bethel, and the change of the patriarch's name at Penuel—demonstrates that this pericope is to be reckoned among the Priestly literature which was composed as alternative to the JE narratives. Just as the Priestly rendition of the Abrahamic covenant in Genesis 17 combines the data of two JE narratives (Genesis 15 and 18) into a single episode, so here the Priestly rendition of the Bethel revelation includes the Penuel event as well. The reason for this alternative composition is clear. Both of the JE narratives which it retells portray revelations which are based upon appearances of angels (or possibly of YHWH himself at Penuel). As we have seen several times, this is out of the question for P. The original independence of this pericope from the Exilic tradent's hand is further confirmed by the presence of a divine self-introduction to Jacob here (35:11). This introduction is appropriate because this is the first meeting of God and Jacob in P. It would make no sense if this passage had been composed by the same tradent who was assembling the combined JEP text of the Priestly work.[105] The doublet of the anointing of the pillar and naming of the place Bethel, appearing here (35:14f.) and in E (28:18; 35:7), likewise confirms the original independence of this Priestly account from the tradent's hand.[106]

Jacob's progeny, Gen. 35:23-26. This list of Jacob's male children repeats the names which are already known from the JE

---

[105] Cf. the discussion of the divine self-introduction to Abraham in Genesis 17, above, pp. 86-87. The addition of the word ʿôd here in 35:9 is the reconciling addition of the Exilic tradent.

[106] Gen. 35:14 has often been regarded as E because of its extreme similarity to 28:18. (Cf. Noth, *HPT*, p. 85; Speiser, *Genesis*, pp. 269ff., with reservations.) The similarity, however, is precisely due to the fact that the two verses are a doublet. 35:14, as it is worded, is integral to its present Priestly context. It would form a pointless repetition of Jacob's action, on the other hand, in E.

accounts. Still, it is unlikely that this is the tradent's summary of the names, because Benjamin is here regarded as having been born in Paddan-Aram along with the other eleven sons. Since the Exilic tradent included the E account of Benjamin's birth in Bethlehem only a few verses earlier (35:16-20), it is hardly likely that he chose to contradict his own text in the adjoining summary. This list therefore pre-dates the Exilic tradent and is apparently a Priestly writer's succinct alternative to the long anecdotal etiologies of the JE sources.

Jacob's return to Isaac, Gen. 35:27. This notice may be the work either of the Exilic tradent or of his Priestly predecessors.

The death of Isaac, Gen. 35:28f. The report of the years of Isaac, 35:28, may derive from the *tôlᵉdōt* book. The report of his death, worded quite like that of Abraham, may come from the hand of the Exilic tradent.

The *tôlᵉdōt* (of) Esau, Genesis 36. The heading is the Priestly tradent's (36:1). The list of wives and children which follows, as noted above, doubles and contradicts the other Priestly report of their names (26:34f; 27:46; 28:9). Both reports are prior to the Exilic tradent. The report of Esau's move to Seir (36:6-8) repeats the JE report (33:16) and is an alternative notice (nearly identical to the Priestly description of the parting of Abraham and Lot, 13:6). The remainder of the chapter is apparently composed of other documents relating to the Edomite genealogies, utilized by the Exilic tradent.

The *tôlᵉdōt* (of) Jacob, Gen. 37:2a. This is the last of the Genesis *tôlᵉdōt* headings, introducing the Joseph cycle of mixed JEP compositions.

Jacob and Joseph, Gen. 37:1; 41:45b,46a; 46:6,7; 47:27b. Separated from the JE narratives of Jacob and Joseph, the Priestly account amounts to barely five verses. These verses, moreover, are very strange indeed. Hardly elaborative, they add almost nothing to the JE account. At the same time they flow together comfortably and suffice as a summary of a story which is already well-known. Given the rigid adherence of all the Priestly compositions which we have observed to the fundamental events of the history of the relations of YHWH and humans, abandoning anecdotal episodes, this abbreviated Priestly account is not as enigmatic as it would first appear. It is in fact no shorter than the Priestly accounts of Lot, the birth of Ishmael, and the birth of Isaac. It is alternative composition, prior to the Exilic tradent.[107]

---

[107] 41:46a may be the Exilic tradent's notation.

The children of Israel who come to Egypt, Gen. 46:8-27. This is one of several genealogies which are headed "And these are the names. . ." which the tradent incorporated into the Priestly work.[108]

The years of Jacob, Gen. 47:28. This report of the patriarch's age, like those of the other patriarchs, may be the Exilic tradent's contribution.

The promotion of Ephraim and Manasseh, Gen. 48:3-6. Jacob's repetition of the divine promise made to him at Bethel and his appointment of Ephraim and Manasseh to the status of their father's generation must be reckoned among the alternative literature of the Exilic tradent's received texts, for Jacob's promotion of Joseph's sons is in conflict with the JE material which follows. In the latter he sees Joseph's sons for the first time and asks, "Who are these?" (48:8) and proceeds to bless them with the protection of an angel (48:16). The Priestly version is surely alternative to this.

The blessing of Jacob, Gen. 49:1-28. The exceedingly old poem[109] of 49:1-27 attaches neatly to the Priestly pericope which follows (49:28-33) and is thus most probably the insertion of the Exilic tradent.[110]

The death of Jacob, Gen. 49:29-33; 50:12f. The account of Jacob's last words, his death, and his burial is an alternative composition to the equivalent JE portrayal, 50:1-11. The last two verses of the Priestly version, 50:12f., flow naturally from the preceding P material but fit their present location badly, repeating the intervening JE account, excluding the Egyptian party which, according to the older source, accompanied the sons of Jacob to Canaan. This Priestly pericope must be reckoned among the received texts of the Priestly tradent.

In both stages of the Priestly work, the Genesis accounts represent a rather limited Priestly scope relative to the JE narrative.

---

[108] See Cross, *CMHE*, pp. 303f.

[109] F.M. Cross and D.N. Freedman, *Studies in Ancient Yahwistic Poetry*, pp. 69f.

[110] See Noth, *HPT*, pp. 14,18n., 84n., 184n. Von Rad claims that "v. 28b is the precise continuation of 49:1a; i.e. the narrative context is interrupted by the insertion of Jacob's blessing." *Genesis*, p. 424. This is questionable, for it leaves the mention of each son's blessing in v. 28b without any referent. The wording of v. 28b, rather, certainly seems to refer back to precisely that which has just transpired, i.e. the individual blessing of the sons.

The Priestly materials constitute a succinct, incomplete, alternative presentation of the content of the JE narrative traditions, more systematically adherent to a directed portrayal of history, less anecdotal, portraying the deity in a more transcendent role. These materials have a preparatory character, pointing toward events to come. The result of the combination of these materials with those to which they are alternative will be discussed following the analysis of the remainder of the Priestly work.

The children of Israel who come to Egypt, Exod. 1:1-5. This list is a summarized version of the list which appears in Gen. 46:8-27. In this Exodus version only the twelve eponymous ancestors of the tribes are named, the names of the succeeding generations being replaced by the single notation that each man came with his household (1:1). Here we surely have before us the work of the Exilic tradent, constructing an introduction to the Egyptian sojourn section of the Priestly work.

The death of Joseph's generation and growth of the people, Exod. 1:6f. This report of the passing of the generation of Joseph and of the subsequent multiplication of the Israelites is a doublet of the JE narrative which immediately follows. Adding no new information to the JE narrative, it is Priestly alternative composition.

God regards Israel's suffering, Exod. 2:23b-25. No portrayal of the oppression appears in the Priestly materials. This pericope begins with the groaning of the Israelites "because of the work." This might conceivably be the tradent's insertion of an elaboration of the JE account of the oppression. If so the tradent drew upon the language of the subsequent Priestly account of the first meeting of YHWH and Moses (6:4f.)[111] and composed its referent here retrospectively. One must admit that this is a difficult literary process to envision and that, therefore, it is more likely that this pericope is another portion of the tradent's received materials. The absence of a Priestly account of the oppression is then to be explained either (1) as having been eliminated in favor of the JE account, or (2) as having consisted of only a short statement which was identical or nearly-identical to a statement in the JE account (e.g. Exod. 1:13), or (3) as further indication that P was not a complete and independent document prior to reaching the hands of the Exilic tradent.

---

[111] This was a received text; see discussion below.

YHWH and Moses, Exod. 6:2-12. The Priestly account of the first meeting of YHWH and Moses is, without a doubt, a Priestly alternative to the JE account of the burning bush meeting. The Priestly account is indeed portraying a *first* meeting and thus apparently was not composed as part of the work of the Exilic tradent who set JE portrayals of two meetings prior to this one. The introduction of the name YHWH here as something new likewise eliminates the possibility that the tradent who handled J composed it. This portrayal of the revelation of the divine name, further, is itself a doublet of the E portrayal of the same revelation at the burning bush (Exod. 3:13-15). Moses' declaration in P that he is of "uncircumcised lips" (6:12) is a doublet of his declaration in the J version that he is of "heavy mouth and heavy tongue" (4:10). In P Moses delivers his message to the people but "they did not listen because of shortness of spirit and because of the hard work" (6:9). This is a direct contradiction of the JE account, in which YHWH tells Moses that the leaders of the people will listen to him (3:18); Moses goes to the people and they do in fact believe him (4:31). The number of doublets and contradictions between this Priestly text and the corresponding JE texts makes it impossible to view the Priestly composition as the work of the tradent who combined it with JE. The JE account, portraying an angel in the burning bush, submerging the E introduction of the divine name in a combination with the non-differentiating J material, was unacceptable to the Priestly writer(s) who engaged in the composition of alternative texts.

Genealogy of Reuben, Simeon, and Levi, Exod. 6:13-30. This pericope reflects the hand of the Priestly tradent elaborating upon received material, in this case a genealogy of the tribal fathers. The tradent has reproduced the list only as far as the tribe of Levi, the apparent intention being to trace the roots of Aaron and Moses. The first verse of this pericope and the concluding three verses (26-28) are clearly the tradent's own inclusio, modeled on the preceding Priestly pericope. The last two verses (29f.) are a particularly clear epanalepsis, repeating 6:11f. Exodus 6 thus provides us with an excellent example of each of the two principal stages of the Priestly work, showing the task of each hand and the appearance of the final product.

Moses and Pharaoh, Exod. 4:21b; 7:1-13,19,20a,21b,22; 8:1-3,11b-15; 9:8-12,35; 10:20,27; 11:9f. The plague traditions of Exodus form one of the most complex constructions of Priestly and JE composition in the Torah. Separated from one another, neither the JE nor the Priestly material flows comfortably. As Cross has pointed out, it is hardly possible to picture the present shape of the section as the basically mechanical juxtaposition of corresponding blocks of two narratives by a redactor.[112] At the same time, analysis of the section does not permit us to view it as layers of Priestly elaboration upon a JE text. There are doublets of entire sections, such as the twin portrayals of the plague of blood.[113] There is the conflicting doublet of the portrayals of the serpent episode in the JE and the Priestly versions. In the JE account Moses' rod is to become a serpent (*nāḥāš*) before the *people* so that they will believe in him (4:1-5); in the Priestly version it is before Pharaoh and his servants that the rod—of Aaron—becomes a serpent (*tannîn*, 7:10). In JE Moses is told that he is as a God *to Aaron* (4:16); in the Priestly version Moses is told that he is as a God *to Pharaoh* (and Aaron is his prophet!), (7:1). There are definitely two originally independent accounts represented here, and yet neither is presently complete, and the two are integrally bound. Upon examination one finds that this construction is the work of the tradent who produced the unified Priestly work. In the plagues narrative one may uncover an editorial framework which, like the *tôlᵉdōt* and Stations frameworks which respectively precede and follow it, gives shape to the materials which it encloses, thus accounting for what is otherwise a thirteen-chapter gap between the two structures which Cross identified. Just as the *tôlᵉdōt* and Stations frameworks are based on received texts which the tradent had at his disposal, so the framework of the plagues section is derivative from a received text, namely: the Priestly account of Moses and Pharaoh. In this account, YHWH informs Moses prior to the latter's first meeting with Pharaoh that "I shall harden Pharaoh's heart. . . and he will not listen to you" (7:3f.). The realization of this prediction is then noted several times in the account of Moses and Pharaoh which follows. Using the verbs *qšh* and-*ḥzq* for "to harden," this is the Priestly alternative to the JE account which regularly uses the verb *kbd* for the hardening of Pharaoh's heart. Examination of each of the appearances of this remark shows that it was the Priestly tradent's hand which structured the work. The episode of Aaron's rod becoming a snake (P) concludes with the Priestly notation,

---

[112] *CMHE*, p. 318.

[113] See Zevit, "The Priestly Redaction and Interpretation of the Plague Narrative in Exodus," p. 199.

"And the heart of Pharaoh was hard (*wyḥzq*), and he did not listen to them, as YHWH had said" (7:13). The description of the blood plague (P and JE combined) concludes identically (7:22). The description of the plague of frogs (P and JE combined) ends with the JE notation that Pharaoh hardened (*hkbd*) his heart (8:11), but attached to this JE statement is the Priestly remainder: ". . . and he did not listen to them, as YHWH had said." The plagues of lice and boils (both wholly P) conclude with the full Priestly statement (8:15; 9:12). The plagues of flies and pestilence (both wholly JE) each conclude with the full JE statement: "And Pharaoh hardened (*kbd*) his heart, and he did not send forth the people" (8:28; 9:7). Thus the plague accounts which are wholly P conclude with the P notation, and those which are wholly JE conclude with the JE notation, and those which are combined conclude with the P notation or with a combined notation. This unsurprising picture changes, however, in the remaining plagues. The plague of hail is entirely a JE composition, yet it concludes with a mixed notation in which the Priestly elements predominate, thus: "And the heart of Pharaoh was hard (*wyḥzq*) and he did not send forth the children of Israel, as YHWH had said" (9:35). A Priestly statement has somehow come to summarize a JE pericope.[114] The lengthy narrative which follows, climaxing in the plague of locusts, likewise is wholly JE, but concludes: And YHWH hardened (*ḥzq*) the heart of Pharaoh, and he did not send forth the people" (10:20). The account of the plague of darkness follows; it, too, is entirely a JE composition, yet it concludes similarly to the two preceding accounts (10:27). There follows a JE portrayal of the last dialogue of Moses and Pharaoh, at the end of which there stands a Priestly conclusion to the entire sequence of Moses/Pharaoh encounters, thus:

> And Moses and Aaron performed all these wonders before Pharaoh, and YHWH hardened (*wyḥzq*) the heart of Pharaoh, and he did not send forth the children of Israel from his land.

> (11:10)

---

[114] The distinction between *ḥzq* and *kbd* is consistently confirmed in the LXX. Note also the doublet of the hardening of Pharaoh's heart in 9:34 (*kbd*) and again in 9:35 (*ḥzq*). *ḥzq lb*, further, continues as a key term in P through the Sea episode; Exod. 14:4,8 (cf. v. 5, JE), 17.

The presence of Priestly conclusions upon JE narratives, fulfilling the prediction which is made in a Priestly summation, indicates that we have in the Exodus account of Moses and Pharaoh portions of two received texts, one P and one JE, which have been combined by the Priestly tradent in a framework which he modeled upon the P version. A final indicator that this is the case is the presence of the Priestly formulation of the hardening-of-the-heart phrase in the midst of the JE burning bush account (4:21b). The context is somewhat awkward as it stands (4:21-23) and apparently reflects the tradent's unifying work. Indeed the specific combination of phrases in this verse, 4:21b, viz. that God will harden (ḥzq) Pharaoh's heart and that Pharaoh will not send forth the people, otherwise occurs only in the four passages which we last observed.

The Passover commands, Exod. 12:1-20,28. The Priestly record of YHWH's instructions on the eve of the final plague is manifestly an alternative to the JE text which follows it. Both command that a lamb be slaughtered (12:6; cf. v. 21), that blood be spread on the doorposts (12:7; cf. v. 22), so that YHWH will pass over (psḥ) the homes prepared thus (12:13; cf. v. 23), and will not permit the destroyer (mašḥît) to enter (Ibid.). It should be noted that in this Priestly composition it is predicted that the firstborn of Egypt are to die, but the fulfillment of this prediction is never portrayed in P. Perhaps this denouement was eliminated in favor of the JE version. In light of the retention of a multitude of doublets which we have seen thus far, however, any such claim of elimination of texts which "must have" existed are tenuous and must therefore be accompanied by substantial supportive evidence. Meanwhile, we must continue to be open to doubts as to whether the alternative Priestly compositions which the Exilic tradent inherited were ever a completed work prior to that tradent's assembly of them, together with the JE sources, into a single Torah.

While considering the Priestly portrayal of the Passover commands, we should consider as well the argument of Kaufmann, mentioned at the outset of Chapter II, that this Priestly treatment prescribes a home sacrifice and must therefore pre-date Josiah and centralization.[115] Kaufmann presumed that this text is prescriptive, commanding home sacrifice and blood on doorposts as an annual holiday observance.[116] The text itself, however, purports to be

---

[115] RI, p. 179.

[116] Noth also sees reflections of actual old observances here; HPT, p. 67.

purely descriptive of the historical event and not prescriptive of the future celebration of that event. The text in fact explicitly declares its prescriptive content to begin at v. 14, i.e. *following* the description of the original exodus meal. The prescriptive section deals with the Passover convocation and unleavened bread only, while the portion which relates to the Passover meal has apparently been severed and relocated by the Priestly tradent to his next section, namely:

The continuation of the Passover commands, Exod. 12:40-51. Following the section which we have just discussed comes the JE account of the last plague and Israel's release. This is followed by the first of the Priestly headings which are based upon the Stations list of Numbers 33. This heading, "And the children of Israel journeyed from Rameses to Succoth" (12:37), introduces a body of JE and Priestly materials. The first verses of the Priestly material (12:40f.) are the Priestly version's statement that Israel left Egypt; these verses are probably part of the Priestly tradent's received materials. The verse which follows, however, is the first evaluative remark to appear in the Priestly materials, thus:

> It is a night of observances to YHWH for bringing them
> out of the land of Egypt; it is this night, observances to
> YHWH, for all the children of Israel for their genera-
> tions.

> (12:42)

This is the first interruption by the narrator into the history. That this verse was composed by the Priestly tradent is suggested from the structure of that which follows. The next verses constitute the prescriptive treatment of the Passover meal which Kaufmann sought above. These verses connect naturally to the end of the Priestly passage which deals with the Passover convocation and the unleavened bread (12:14-20). One should note that this prescriptive treatment of the meal differs from the portrayal of the meal which took place in Egypt (12:1-13) in precisely the two details which interested Kaufmann, namely the home slaughter of the animal and the spreading of its blood on the doorposts. Neither of these actions is required in the prescriptive passage before us. The claim that the Priestly view of Passover is pre-centralization, there-fore, is unfounded. The Passover meal command now concludes, followed by two editorial connectors which must be the work of the Priestly tradent. The first (12:50) states that "All the children of

Israel did as YHWH had commanded Moses and Aaron, so they did." This is a *verbatim* repetition of the Priestly remark which concludes the previous section (12:28). The second editorial notation (12:51) is the statement that Israel left Egypt; it is the tradent's epanalepsis, comparable to 12:40f. Thus he enclosed the material which he inserted here.

The Sea, Exod. 13:20; 14:1-4,8,9b,10ac,15-18,21ac,22,23,26,-27a,28,29; 15:19. The account of the splitting of the Sea is introduced with a second heading which derives from the Stations list (13:20) and is part of the tradent's framework. The conclusion of the account, 15:19, is cast in the language of the Priestly version and is an epanalepsis following the Song of the Sea (15:1-18).[117] Clearly an editorial device of unification, it, too, is to be attributed to the Priestly tradent. All of the Priestly material which stands between these two verses is a composition which was prior to the tradent. If this material is separated from the J and E materials with which it is bound, the P and J accounts each flow as a complete and unified composition. (E is incomplete.) The doublets are numerous. At the same time, the angel of the JE account is eliminated in P. This Priestly text is thus an alternative composition combined with the JE texts in the second stage of the Priestly work.

Provision of manna and quail, Exod. 16:1-3,6-35a,36. The first verse of this pericope is another of the tradent's headings from the Numbers 33 Station list. The Priestly alternative to the JE accounts which appear in this chapter (16:4f.,35b) and in a subsequent wilderness episode (Num. 11:4-34). Exod. 16:35 contains a blatant doublet from the two versions. The similarity of 16:4b,28 to common Deuteronomistic phrases has led Noth to regard them as Deuteronomistic supplements to the JE narrative.[118] It is at least as likely that v. 28 is simply P—as its place in context suggests—using a favorite phrase of the Deuteronomist, consciously or unconsciously. The similarity of v. 4 to D is not surprising in light of the fact that this is one of the many JE passages on which D directly depends; cf. Deut. 8:2,16.

---

[117] On the Song, see Cross, "The Song of the Sea and Canaanite Myth," *CMHE*, pp. 112-144.

[118] *HPT*, p. 31n. Other Dtr supplements, according to Noth, are Exod. 12:24-27a; 13:1-16; 15:25b,26; 19:3b-9; 32:7-14.

The journey from Sin to Rephidim, Exod. 17:1. This is another of the Exilic tradent's Station headings, introducing a body of JE narrative.

The arrival at Sinai, Exod. 19:1,2a. As discussed above, these two verses exhibit a doublet, 19:1 being the Priestly notation of the arrival at Sinai, 19:2 being the heading derived from the Stations list.

The Decalogue, Exod. 20:1-17. The Priestly reworked version of the Decalogue is manifestly an alternative to the Deuteronomistic reworked version (Deut. 5:6-18). This is apparent in the respective explanations of the Sabbath command. The Priestly version attaches the Sabbath to the seven-day creation in characteristic P language (Exod. 20:8-11; cf. 31:12-17 and Genesis 1). The Deuteronomistic version predicates the Sabbath observance upon the release from Egyptian servitude (Deut. 5:12-15).[119] The Exodus Decalogue text is thus to be reckoned among the Priestly alternative literature which the Exilic tradent received.

The cloud and the glory on Mount Sinai, Exod. 24:15b-18a. This pericope is clearly a Priestly alternative expression of the JE portrayal of the Sinai theophany, Exod. 19:18-20. In the JE version,

> Mount Sinai smoked entirely because YHWH descended upon it in fire. . . and YHWH called Moses to the top of the mountain, and Moses went up.

In the Priestly version,

> The glory of YHWH settled ($škn$)[120] upon Mount Sinai, and the cloud covered it for six days; and he called to Moses on the seventh day from the midst of the cloud. . . and Moses came into the midst of the cloud, and he went up to the mountain.

The two passages describe the same event, but the Priestly writer has recast the description of that event in his own specialized vocabulary. The smoke in the JE version has become the cloud in the

---

[119] See above, Chapter I, pp. 31-32, discussion of the emphatic concern of Dtr[1] for Egypt. Cf. Mowinckel, *Erwägungen zur Pentateuch Quellenfrage*, p. 32

[120] Or "tented;" see Cross, *CMHE*, pp. 298ff., 322.

Priestly composition. Instead of YHWH's personal descent in the JE account, the glory of YHWH settled (*škn*) on the mount in P. This Priestly version of the theophany and Moses' ascent has been attached by the Exilic tradent to the JE account of Moses' second ascent of Sinai. The Priestly pericope is enclosed in an epanalepsis, repeating the words "And Moses went up to the mountain" (24:15,18), which is the unifying device of the tradent.

The Tabernacle (ark, etc.) instruction, Exod. 25-31:11. As discussed above, this document is necessarily pre-Exilic. It may have been composed at any time from the first pitching of the Tabernacle to the period between Josiah and Exile. Whatever the date of composition, however, it most certainly played a crucial part among the Priestly compositions of the latter period, when the Tabernacle became the key Priestly expression of centralization of worship.

The Sabbath command, Exod. 31:12-17. Primarily elaborative, independent of the material which precedes and follows it, this emphatic supplement to the Sabbath commandment is probably the tradent's addition to the received texts.

Moses' receipt of the tablets, 31:18. This is the Priestly version of a JE tradition (cf. 32:15f.) and therefore most probably should be associated with the Priestly alternative compositions.

The vail of Moses, Exod. 34:29-35. This difficult text is thought generally to be purely P, and by Noth to be a Priestly reworking of a JE text.[121] The latter view seems to derive from the feeling that the shining face of Moses, which must be covered with a vail, is not the sort of image which one generally finds in P. Atypical it is; but that is hardly sufficient evidence to deny its place in the Priestly corpus, which is amply supported by numerous familiar Priestly terms, the contextually gratuitous references to Aaron, and the integral tie between this account and the material which precedes and follows it. The last Priestly notice which precedes it (31:18) states that Moses finished speaking with YHWH and took the tablets in his hand. Now Moses descends with the tablets and, after covering his face, reports all the things which YHWH has commanded (34:32,34). This in turn anticipates the following Priestly composition, in which Moses begins his report of the

---

121 W. Beyerlin, *Origins and History of the Oldest Sinaitic Traditions*, p. 3; Carpenter and Harford-Battersby, *The Hexateuch*, p. 35; Cross, *CMHE*, p. 314; Noth, *HPT*, p. 31n.; *Exodus*, p. 267.

Tabernacle, ark, etc. instructions with the words, "This is the thing which YHWH has commanded" (35:4). Though we may admit the possibility that this is an extremely well constructed transition composed by the Exilic tradent, its tie with the contexts of the adjacent received texts is so integral as to suggest its original unity with them.

The execution of the Tabernacle (ark, etc.) instruction, Exodus 35-40. Like the earlier Tabernacle document (Exod. 25-31:11), on which it depends, this composition must be reckoned as a fundamental unit of the pre-Exilic Priestly literature. We have already noted the relationship of its concluding description of Moses' inability to enter the Tent of Meeting (40:35) to the Deuteronomistic description of the priests' inability to enter the Temple on its dedication day (1 Kings 8:11). The three verses which follow constitute a Priestly expression of the manner in which YHWH's cloud governs Israel's journeys. This is an alternative portrayal to the JE description of this phenomenon (Exod. 13:21f.). The three-verse notice breaks its context, which continues in Leviticus 8, and so it was either intended as a parenthetical remark or was relocated to this position by the Priestly tradent.

Sacrificial law, Leviticus 1-7. The manual of offerings which appears here may reflect long-established sacrificial law. This particular formulation, nonetheless, derives from the period between centralization and Exile. Noth, in opposition to the widely-accepted opinion that this text is post-Exilic, has argued that it must derive from the period of the monarchy in light of its lack of concern with the Levites.[122] Our investigations into the place of the Tabernacle provide even stronger evidence that this text must pre-date the destruction,—and be later than centralization. The centrality of the Tabernacle to the entire scheme of the manual of offerings is manifest in the multiplicity of references to the Tent of Meeting which occur throughout (1:1,3,5; 3:2,8,13; 4:4,5,7,14,16,18; 6:9,19,23). As discussed above, this emphasis upon the Tabernacle as the only legitimate site of sacrificial worship is inconceivable after 587. It must fall between centralization and Exile. The response of Jeremiah to this specific Priestly section on sacrificial law, discussed above,[123] further supports this conclusion. Our previous discussion of the treatment of national sin through ignorance in this section

---

[122] *The Laws in the Pentateuch*, p. 8.

[123] pp. 74-76.

(Lev. 4:13-21) also argues the post-Josianic and pre-Exilic composition of the section.

The investment of Aaron, Leviticus 8,9. The centrality of the Tabernacle once again in this portrayal of the consecration of the Priesthood, together with the clear assignment of the priestly prerogatives only to Aaron and his sons, points to the concerns of the Aaronid priests of the period between centralization and Exile, i.e. the time when the Aaronids were favorable to the advantages of centralized worship but not favorable to sharing their prerogatives with members of any other priestly house (e.g. the Mushites). The description of the fire which falls from YHWH and of the people's response has been discussed above as being comparable to the portrayal of Elijah on Carmel in the Deuteronomistic history.[124] It should be noted that these chapters continue the Tabernacle account of Exodus 40. The manual of offerings, Leviticus 1-7, was inserted in the midst of this divided unit so as to precede Aaron's first sacrifice with the corpus of sacrificial law. The reference to the anointing of Aaron in 7:35f., as Noth has pointed out, anticipates the portrayal of the investment of Aaron in the following chapters.[125] These two verses are to be traced to the tradent who assembled these separate compositions in the Priestly work. The recognition of separate Priestly compositions here is itself to be emphasized as cautioning us once again against concluding that the Priestly literature was a unified source prior to reaching the desk of the Exilic tradent.

The death of Nadab and Abihu; the charge to Aaron and his sons, Leviticus 10. In the absence of an understanding of the motivation which generated this enigmatic account, it is difficult to determine at which stage of the Priestly work it was composed. A charge to Aaron and his sons, which places upon them the responsibility of teaching to Israel the statutes which YHWH has given through Moses, is embedded in this account. This charge is associated with the Tent of Assembly (10:9) and describes the teaching task of the priests as related to the separation between clean and unclean, between holy and profane (10:10). The Tent reference points to pre-Exilic composition, as does the latter matter, which we have already observed to pre-date Ezekiel.[126] The emphasis here

[124] See above, pp. 67-68.

[125] *HPT*, p. 8.

[126] See above, p. 76.

upon the charge that the Aaronids are to be the appointed teachers of Torah is all-important, further suggesting the derivation of this composition from the time in which competing priestly houses each claimed that role.

Law of clean and unclean, Lev. 11-15. Like the sacrificial law, these statutues may be quite old, i.e. prior even to the first of the two stages of the Priestly work which we examine here. The list of permitted and forbidden animals which appears here (Leviticus 11) is an earlier formulation than the Deuteronomic version, as William L. Moran has shown.[127] The purity laws which follow may derive from comparably early origins, but their present formulations are tied to the compositions of the years between centralization and Exile by their setting the required purification rituals at the Tabernacle (12:6; 14:11,23; 15:14,29,31).

Ritual of the Day of Atonement, Leviticus 16. The Tabernacle is central to the entire Day of Atonement proceedings, and the text especially emphasizes that the ritual described here is the law *forever* (16:29,31,34). This demand can only have been made prior to 587. I have also argued above that the origin of the Autumnal New Year and Day of Atonement must have pre-dated Exile because of the impossibility of initiation of major holidays as direct response to the event of Exile with subsequent ascription of the innovations to Moses. Leviticus 16 must necessarily be pre-Exilic.

The Holiness Code, Leviticus 17-26. Again we may be dealing with old statutes, but their formulation in this particular legal corpus, combined with post-centralization materials, is clearly to be reckoned to the same age as that of the preceding section: post-centralization and pre-destruction. As noted above, the association of the Holiness Code and Deuteronomy has been recognized before. Wellhausen called the Holiness Code "the transition from Deuteronomy to the Priestly Code."[128] Wellhausen had to admit that the centralization law of Leviticus 17 does not merely "presuppose" the Deuteronomistic centralization. It demands it no less emphatically than does Deuteronomy. Kaufmann, as summarized above, argued that if Leviticus 17 refers to a single place of sacrifice, then "the law in effect bans the eating of meat for the bulk of the people, who were unable to bring their animals to the

---

[127] See above, p. 71, n. 64.

[128] *PHI*, p. 35n.; see his discussion, pp. 376ff. Noth also discusses the relationship of the two corpora; *The Laws in the Pentateuch*, pp. 8,13,23-26.

Jerusalem temple for sacrificial slaughter."[129] He therefore associated the law—and the Tabernacle—with widespread local sanctuaries. The Priestly centralization law, however, has no such consequence. Leviticus 17 requires only that oxen, sheep, and goats be slaughtered at the central place. Game and fowl are permitted for slaughter anywhere, and the people are bound in any event by both D and P to come to Jerusalem at least three times a year for festival sacrifice. Certainly the flesh of an entire ox which was sacrificed on Passover sufficed a family's meat consumption until Shavuot. Kaufmann denied the presence of the thrice-annual pilgrimage law in P, but this denial is *ex hypothesis* from his prior conclusion that the Tabernacle in P does not refer to the central pilgrimage place. We may safely conclude that Leviticus 17 derives from the years between centralization and Exile. Other portions of the Holiness Code—beside the Deuteronomistic association which Wellhausen and Noth have demonstrated—likewise exhibit evidence of composition in this period. Reference to the Tabernacle in the mixed laws of Leviticus 19 (v. 21) and to the *pārōket* in the Priestly laws of Leviticus 21 (v. 23) point to this period, as does the inclusion of the Autumnal New Year and Day of Atonement in the holiday list of Leviticus 23. The inclusion, among the covenant blessings, of the promise that the Tabernacle will be in Israel's midst *in the land* likewise points to pre-Exilic composition. The bulk of the Holiness Code must be regarded as pre-Exilic Priestly literature, i.e. it must be reckoned among the received texts of the tradent of the Priestly work. Small units within this corpus may of course be later. The instruction to build booths on the festival of Sukkot (Lev. 23:39-42), for example, is unconnected to the section of this chapter which deals with Sukkot, which concludes in 23:36. The booth instruction comes after the obvious conclusion of the festival pericope in 23:37. The matter of booths on Sukkot appears again in Neh. 8:13-18. According to that narrative, Ezra and the returned Jews find in the Torah of Moses the command to build booths on Sukkot. The names of species of trees to be used in the booths in Neh. 8:15 confirms the tie between this text and the Leviticus 23 Sukkot instruction, which includes a similar list of species in 23:40.[130] The text in Nehemiah specifically notes that this instruction had never been performed in Israel since the days

---

[129] *RI*, pp. 180f.

[130] Note the scribal change of *hădās* in Neh. for *hādār* in Leviticus.

of Joshua (8:17). This suggests that the booth instruction was not instituted together with the other festival laws, just as it was clearly composed separately. The passage referring to booths in Leviticus 23 therefore must be an Exilic composition. Kaufmann argued the opposite, i.e. that dwelling in booths was a pre-centralization observance.[131] He failed to explain the specific statement to the contrary in Neh. 8:17, i.e. that this had never been done since the days of Joshua.

The inclusion of the curse of Exile in the curst list of Leviticus 26 does not necessarily demand an Exilic dating.[132] The promises of restoration in the event of repentance, 26:39-45, however, probably are an Exilic addition to be traced to the hand of the Priestly tradent.

Appendix on dedicatory gifts, Leviticus 27. It is difficult to determine in which stage of the Priestly work this text belongs.[133]

Census, Numbers 1. Cross has identified several portions of the book of Numbers as old documents which the Priestly tradent in Exile introduced into the Priestly work. These include the list of the $n^e\acute{s}\hat{i}\hat{i}m$ in 1:5-16 and the census role in 1:17-47.[134] The introductory statement (1:1-4) is presumably the Priestly tradent's own setting for the lists. The closing treatment of the special role of the Levites, explaining their non-inheritance of land, ties them specifically to the Tabernacle. It is a Priestly alternative to the Deuteronomistic treatment of the same matter (Deut. 1:9; Josh. 18:7), which assigns them the Priesthood in place of land. As an alternative composition in which the Tabernacle is integral, this Priestly composition is to be reckoned among the pre-Exilic materials.

Arrangement of the camp, Numbers 2-4. These chapters contain more statistical lists which the tradent assembled.[135] The $t\hat{o}l^ed\bar{o}t$ heading of Num. 3:1, though not serving the framing function of the previous examples, is an editorial introduction to the genealogy of Aaron which follows. The Levitic organization which is the

---

[131] *RI*, p. 179.

[132] See Chapter I, p. 36n.

[133] See Noth's discussion, *Leviticus*, pp. 203-208.

[134] *CMHE*, p. 321; cf. Noth, *Numbers*, pp. 11,20f.

[135] Cross, *CMHE*, p. 321.

subject of the remainder of Numbers 3 and 4 pictures the Levites in terms of their position and responsibilities toward the Tabernacle. It is pre-Exilic.

Lepers, trespass and recompense, Num. 5:1-10. These two short matters offer little evidence on which to determine the stage of the Priestly work to which each belongs.

The suspected adulteress, Num. 5:11-31. This law requires the existence of the Tabernacle for execution. It is pre-Exilic.

The nazirite, Num. 6:1-21. This law likewise culminates in a sacrifice at the Tabernacle (6:13,18) and is thus pre-Exilic.

The priestly blessing, Num. 6:22-27. The blessing offers little ground for dating.[136]

Tribal offerings, Numbers 7. This old list[137] is cast as a portrayal of the tribes' dedicatory donations for the Tabernacle (7:1,89). It is one of the tradent's received texts.

Dedication of the Levites, Numbers 8. Once again the interests of the Aaronids between the time of centralization and Exile are apparent. The position which is assigned to the Levites in this pericope is alternative to the Priestly role which the Deuteronomistic literature conceives. The fundamental attachment of their role to the Tabernacle in this text makes its purpose and its time of origin clear.

Celebration of Passover, Num. 9:1-14. The observance of the second anniversary of the exodus, as portrayed here, is at the same time the culmination of the dedication of the Tabernacle.[138] That this pericope is pre-Exilic is suggested not only by its apparent continuation of the development of the Passover observance from other pre-Exilic compositions (Exodus 12), but also by its comparison, in v. 14, of the *gēr* to a "native of the land." The latter is an unlikely choice of wording for an Exilic writer to make as a means of speaking of an Israelite by birth. Indeed, all previous occurrences of the expression "native of the land" appear in passages which we have already identified as pre-Exilic on separate grounds (Exod. 12:19,49; Lev. 16:29; 17:15; 24:16,22).[139]

---

136 See Noth, *Numbers*, pp. 57f.

137 See Cross, *CMHE*, p. 321.

138 Cross, *CMHE*, p. 84n.

139 Ezekiel uses the term "native" as well (Ezek. 47:22) but it appears in a vision of a

The cloud over the Tabernacle, Num. 9:15-23. The lengthy P legislation which begins at Leviticus 1 now concludes with what might be termed an elaborating epanalepsis of the passage which precedes the legislation (Exod. 40:36-38). The role of the cloud over the Tabernacle as governing the journeys of Israel is repeated. This time there is an additional remark, pointing out that depending on the duration of the cloud's rest, the people might tarry at one of the stations of their journey for a matter of days or months or even years (Num. 9:19-23). This emphasis seems clearly designed to enhance the literary structure which the Exilic tradent developed from the Stations list, framing JE and Priestly episodes with the order of the journeys of Israel. At the same time, this pericope resumes the account of Israel's movements which is interrupted at Leviticus 1. The pericope is thus an editorial composition of the Exilic tradent which is pivotal to his creation of a unified Priestly work.

The trumpets of assembly, Num. 10:1-10. The assignment of the sounding of the silver trumpets to the Aaronids for the purpose of assembly at the Tent of Meeting on festivals and in crisis is an eternal command (10:8). It is to be traced to a time when the Tabernacle was still standing, i.e. prior to the destruction and Exile.

Departure from Sinai, Num 10:11-28. This list of tribal leaders is another use of the $n^e\hat{s}i^{\hat{i}}im$ document by the Priestly tradent.[140] The tradent's own hand is apparent in the epanalepsis of v. 13, which resumes the wording of 9:23. The concluding remark of v. 28, "These are the journeys of the children of Israel by their hosts, and they journeyed," is also the work of the tradent, drawing these words directly from the introduction to the Stations list in Num. 33:1. Clearly, the development of the journey as the unifying motif of the accounts of the wilderness years is central to the literary task of the Exilic tradent.

The spies, Num. 13:1-16,21,25,26,32,33; 14:1a,2,3,5-10,26-

---

rebuilt land. One may argue that the Priestly text of Numbers 9 likewise is an Exilic composition in preparation for restoration. The Passover law, however, applied to Jews even when outside of their land (see 9:10). It was therefore of current, and not preparatory, interest to the Exiles. As such, the expression of the law in terms of "natives of the land" remains an unlikely choice of wording for a Babylonian Jew, especially of the second or third generation.

[140] Cross, *CMHE*, p. 321.

38. The Priestly account of the spies is without doubt an alternative composition to the JE and Deuteronomistic portrayals of the event. We have already noted the adoption in P of the Deuteronomic terms "little ones will be a prey" and "evil generation."[141] We note further that when the Priestly and JE materials of Num 13,14 are separated the Priestly version flows as a complete and united whole. In the portrayal of the verdict of YHWH the blatancy of the doublet is undeniable (14:11-25 = J; 26-35 = P). The JE text begins with the rhetorical "how long. . ." (Hebrew: *ᶜad 'ānāh*); the Priestly version begins with a variation of the same expression (Hebrew: *ᶜad mātay*). The JE text climaxes with the standard oath formula of a monotheistic deity: *ḥay 'ānî*, P climaxes in an oath which commences with the same formula and expresses the same verdict, viz. the death of the offending generation. P shares with the JE account the description of the land as "flowing with milk and honey" (13:27; 14:8) as well. Most conclusive, however, is the treatment of Joshua in the Priestly version of the episode. In the JE account, the only survivor of the sentence of YHWH out of the entire nation is the one spy who opposes the evil report of the others, namely Caleb. In Deuteronomy as well, Caleb alone survives because of his merit in this matter (Deut. 1:35f.). Joshua, in JE and in D, survives as the successor to Moses on other merits (Deut. 1:38). The special merit of Joshua is clear in the JE narrative. Joshua alone out of the whole people is dissociated from the incident of the golden calf, as he rather awaits Moses on Sinai (Exod. 24:13; 32:17). Joshua, further, remains in the Tabernacle where YHWH communicates with Moses (Exod. 33:11). But these two sources of Joshua's merit in JE belong to precisely the two subjects which offended the Aaronid priests most. The role in which JE casts Aaron in the matter of the golden calf is an outrage to the Aaronids, and the presence of a non-Aaronid (not even a Levite) in the Tabernacle is a crime punishable by death in P. The Priestly assignment of Joshua to the episode of the spies is thus an alternative to the JE narrative. It is a Priestly writer's solution to the problem that he could not portray the merit of Joshua along the JE lines, and yet he could not deny the place of Joshua in Israel's national tradition as the successor of Moses. The Priestly account of the spies is thus a separate and alternative portrayal to that of the JE sources and not merely an expansion of it. It is to be reckoned among the received texts of the Priestly tradent.

---

[141] Above, pp. 68-69.

Additional sacrificial law, Num. 15:1-31. That this pericope is exceedingly difficult to date is acknowledged by Noth, who still maintains that it is one of the latest portions of the Pentateuch.[142] Its unusual location between wilderness accounts may support Noth's characterization of the material as supplementary. Stronger support of the late composition of this sacrificial legislation lies in the differences between it and the previous sacrificial law. We have observed that the sacrificial law of Lev. 1-7,17 is utterly tied to the Tabernacle, and this fact has led us to the conclusion that that legal corpus must derive from the pre-Exilic years. In Numbers 15 we are confronted with a second corpus which deals anew with regular sacrifice, holiday sacrifice, sacrifices of vow, and individual and national sacrifices for sin through error, adding cereal and drink offerings. In this repetitious corpus, however, there is not a single reference to the Tabernacle. The absence of mention of the Tabernacle in a legislative text which otherwise duplicates Priestly laws of sacrifice is no coincidence. This second corpus of sacrificial law must be an Exilic composition. Now that the Tabernacle had been destroyed, the Priestly tradent in Exile could only express sacrificial law in general terms when writing with an eye toward restoration. Indeed, this pericope may have been composed precisely for the purpose of easing the problem of the extent to which the Tabernacle references pervaded the received texts. In any event, the absence of the Tabernacle here in a text which is already regarded as Exilic on other grounds and which is repetitious of the Leviticus texts which we have found to be pre-Exilic (as Noth has, again on other grounds[143]) adds support in turn to the original notion that the Tabernacle was present in the First Temple until the destruction and was of central importance to the pre-Exilic stage of Priestly composition.

A case of a Sabbath violation, Num. 15:32-36. It is difficult to assign this short episode to a stage of the Priestly work.

Fringes on apparel, Num. 15:37-40. The command to place fringes on the corners of one's garments in P is alternative to the same instruction in Deut. 22:12 and thus most probably derives from the period in which the other alternative texts which we have examined were composed, i.e. prior to the destruction.

---

[142] *Numbers*, p. 114; *HPT*, p. 9.

[143] See discussion above, p. 102.

The rebellion of Korah, Num. 16:1a,2b-11,16-24,27a,32b,35.
As the commentaries on the book of Numbers readily admit, the
combined JE and Priestly account of the rebellion of Dathan,
Abiram, Korah, and two hundred fifty men of reknown—as it
appears in Numbers 16 and is recalled in Num. 26:9-11 and Deut.
11:6[144] —is one of the most complex literary conflations in the
Torah.[145] It does not separate into two complete, flowing narratives.
As Cross has pointed out, it cannot, therefore, be explained as a
redactor's piecework of blocks of narrative material.[146] The present
combination of texts, further, is so disjointed as to leave the action
taking place at two locations simultaneously: at the tents of Korah,
Dathan, and Abiram (16:24,27) and at the Tent of Meeting (v. 19).
In the present combination, also, Korah's company is at the same
time a group of Israelite leaders from no single tribe (v. 2) and a
group of Levites seeking priesthood (vv. 8-10). They perish both
in the earthquake (v. 32) and again in the divine fire (v. 35).
(There is oddly no notice that Korah himself perishes.) The
Priestly account thus cannot be an expansion of the JE narrative by
the Priestly tradent. No less baffling than this question of the
manner of their combination is the question of why the two stories
(JE and Priestly) were combined at all. The recognition of two
stages in the Priestly work may help to explain the literary process
which produced this text. We have seen that nearly every one of
the received accounts of the Exilic tradent is an alternative composition to some JE account. The Priestly account of Korah, however, has no equivalent in JE. It is conceivable that the original
Priestly author of this episode sought to compose a story which
would declare the priestly prerogatives of the Aaronids as opposed
to the Levites, but, lacking a tradition on which to base this composition, that Priestly author turned the JE account of Dathan and
Abiram into such a story and added a Levite who was known from
tradition, namely Korah, to their company as its leader. The Exilic
tradent thus would have received a JE account of Dathan and
Abiram and a Priestly account of Dathan, Abiram, and Korah. The
overlapping and contradiction of two such stories would present a
far more complex editorial problem to the tradent than any of the

[144] See also Ps. 106:17.

[145] Noth, *Numbers*, pp. 120-129; Jacob Liver, "Korah, Dathan and Abiram," *Scripta Hierosolymitana* 8, pp. 189-217.

[146] *CMHE*, pp. 315, 318.

accounts which we have seen thus far. The result would be the complex text which we have before us. The attempt to explain the present state of Numbers 16 in this way is admittedly speculative, but two references to Dathan and Abiram in the midst of P clauses (16:25,27a) and one reference to Korah in the midst of a JE context (16:32b) support the notion. One cannot simply attribute these references to the reconciling hand of the tradent, because the reference to Korah in 16:32b does not reconcile matters at all, but rather creates the blatant contradiction of v. 35 discussed above, i.e. the double death of Korah's company.[147]

The entire focus of the Korah account on the issue of who is holy has been discussed above in terms of response to the Deuteronomistic contention that holiness devolves upon the entire people.[148] This character of response in the Priestly account further points to its origin in the years which produced the many other Priestly alternative texts.

Aaronids and Levites, Numbers 17,18. These chapters contain materials which relate to the central issue of the Korah account, i.e. the relative prerogatives of the Aaronids and Levites. The bronze censers of Korah's company are made into a covering of the altar as a reminder that no one who is not an Aaronid may offer incense, "that he be not like Korah and his company" (17:5).[149] A plague which attacks the congregation as YHWH's response to their complaint that Moses and Aaron have killed "people of YHWH" is then arrested by Aaron's use of incense (17:11f.). The special place of the tribe of Levi is then confirmed by the miraculous blossoming of its tribal staff, on which the name of Aaron is inscribed. The chapter then concludes with the declaration of the people that whoever comes near to the Tabernacle will die (17:28). In the following chapter the Aaronids are assigned the responsibility

---

[147] Some commentators see here two originally separate Priestly Korah accounts, one recounting the Levites' challenge, one dealing with the two hundred fifty men of reknown. This view of course also must lead one to acknowledge two separate stages—composition and combination—in the Priestly work.

[148] See above, pp. 69-70.

[149] Liver claims that the matter of the bronze altar covering is secondary because, according to Exod. 27:2, the altar was so covered from the beginning. This claim necessarily presumes that the Tabernacle document and the Korah account are the work of the same author. This presumption is groundless. Liver, "Korah, Dathan and Abiram," p. 191.

of the Tabernacle, the Levites are assigned to the service of the Aaronids, and all others are warned not to approach the Tabernacle on pain of death (18:4,7,22).[150] All of these accounts, assignments, and injunctions serve the purpose of delineating the respective roles of (Aaronid) priest, Levite, and Israelite; and the development of this delineation is utterly tied to the Tabernacle. These materials necessarily derive from the period when the Tabernacle was standing and the Aaronids were expressing by it their autonomy over the centralized Judean worship. The texts are thus to be dated between centralization and Exile.

The red heifer, Numbers 19. The presence of the Tabernacle is once again assumed in this text and is required for execution of the legislation, and the text specifically notes twice that this is the law forever (19:10,21). This law may again have quite early roots,[151] but the present formulation is a product of the years between centralization and Exile.

Water from the rock, Num 20:1-13. An itinerary notice from the Stations list opens this chapter in which the Exilic tradent has gathered Priestly and JE materials. The story of Moses and Aaron at the rock in Meribah is a Priestly reworked doublet of the JE version of this episode in Exod. 17:1-7.[152] The beneficial act of Moses in the JE version becomes the ultimate disobedient act of Moses and Aaron in the Priestly account. This Priestly account is alternative to both JE and Deuteronomy. Deuteronomy attaches the punishment of Moses, viz. that he is to die before reaching the land, to the matter of the spies. The death of Aaron is unexplained in Deuteronomy, where he is mentioned only twice: to report his death and to associate him with the golden calf. The Priestly account now sets the two figures on equal footing in their most critical moment. At the same time the Priestly version abandons features of the JE account which were unacceptable in the Priestly perspective. In the JE version of the striking of the rock, the offense of the people is explicitly "their trying YHWH, saying: 'Is YHWH in our midst or not?'" (Exod. 17:7b). The question of whether YHWH is in the people's midst prior to the construction of the Tabernacle is senseless to P. In P, YHWH is never portrayed as "in the midst" (*bqrb*

---

[150] Contra the portrayal of Joshua in JE and of Samuel in Dtr.

[151] See Noth, *Numbers*, pp. 10, 139.

[152] Cross, *CMHE*, pp. 311,315; Noth, *Numbers*, p. 144.

or *btwk*) of the nation until the Tabernacle is erected. That this is intentional is clear from the explicit P statements attaching his presence in their midst to the institution of the Tabernacle (Exod. 25:8; 29:45f.). Equally unacceptable to P must have been the JE portrayal of YHWH as standing on the rock in front of Moses as the latter strikes it. In the Priestly version, therefore, the time and place of the episode and the attitude toward the immanence of YHWH are changed. It is most unlikely that the hand which took the pains of creating an alternate version of this account was the hand of the Exilic tradent who included it along with the older, unsatisfactory version in the combined Priestly work. The Priestly version of the account of the striking of the rock must be counted, therefore, among the received texts of the Exilic tradent, composed among the alternative texts of the first stage of the Priestly work.

The death of Aaron, Num. 20:22-29. Another itinerary notice (20:22) heads the account of the death of Aaron. This account is tied in detail to the previous Priestly pericope and is the Aaronids' alternative to the Deuteronomic report of the death of their ancestor. It is most probably to be reckoned to the same stage of Priestly composition as that of the preceding pericope.

Itinerary notices, Num. 21:10f.; 22:1. These are the last of the Priestly tradent's twelve headings in the itinerary framework.

Phinehas, Num. 25:6-19. While the separation of the Priestly and JE portions of Numbers 25 presents no particular difficulty, the manner of their combination is one of the most perplexing problems of literary criticism.[153] The JE text (25:1-5) begins a story of the seduction of the Israelites at Baal-Peor by Moabite women, leading to worship of Moabite gods, which is about to end in multiple executions when the story abruptly breaks off. This story without an ending is suddenly continued by a story without a beginning, the latter in the style of P. In the Priestly text, an Israelite brings a Midianite woman apparently into the Tabernacle[154] before his people, who are weeping for some unknown reason at the Tabernacle. In one of the more vivid images in literature, Phinehas kills both offenders in a single action. This action arrests a hitherto unmentioned plague. Phinehas is rewarded with an eternal covenant of priesthood. Neither story is complete; and the second

---

153 Cross *CMHE*, pp. 201-203, 316; Noth, *Numbers*, pp. 195-199.

154 On the meaning of *qubbāh*, see Cross, "The Priestly Tabernacle," pp. 218f.

introduces new elements (the weeping of the congregation,[155] the plague) in a manner which clearly presumes their prior presence, and so this second story cannot be a Priestly elaboration of the JE account. The Priestly account has to have been an originally independent account whose beginning has been removed by the Exilic tradent for the purpose of combination with the JE text. The Priestly account, further, is concerned with Midianites rather than Moabites, a substitution which may well derive from Mushite and Aaronid antagonism, the Aaronid Priestly writer here disparaging the marriage of Moses to a Midianite.[156] Noth has described the Priestly material here as a "secondary supplement to the already completed Pentateuch" on the grounds that it reflects a *post-Exilic* concern with the legitimacy of the Aaronid line, (he says the same of the Korah account).[157] This fails to account, however, for the missing beginning of the Priestly text; and we have seen, in any event, ample evidence that the rivalry of the Priestly houses was strong in the pre-Exilic years, while there is little evidence of it in the post-Exilic period. The Priestly text then is an Aaronid alternative version of the JE story of Baal-Peor and is a received text of the Priestly tradent.

Census, Numbers 26. This census list, like that of Numbers 1, is apparently an old document which the Exilic tradent introduced into the Priestly work.[158] The special notation with regard to Dathan and Abiram, 26:9f., is particularly interesting as an editorial device of the Exilic tradent. Drawing on both the JE and Priestly accounts of Numbers 16, the text is a forthright identification of Dathan and Abiram as members of the party of Korah. Both the earthquake and the fire of Numbers 16 are recalled. There is no other case in the Pentateuch of such an outright reference to a JE narrative by a Priestly writer. At the same time, the matter of Dathan, Abiram, and Korah was precisely the most problematic text for the Priestly tradent with regard to the promulgation of the

---

[155] It is interesting to note that the last Priestly text prior to this one is the account of the death of Aaron, which concludes with the words, "And the whole congregation saw that Aaron had died, and the whole house of Israel *wept* for Aaron thirty days," (20:29). It is conceivable that prior to reaching the Exilic tradent's hands these two pericopes followed one another.

[156] Cf. Cross, *CMHE*, pp. 201-203.

[157] *HPT*, pp. 16,75,196; *UGS*, pp. 201ff., 217.

[158] See Cross, *CMHE*, p. 321; and Noth , *Numbers*, p. 11.

Priestly work. Since the two accounts which are combined here involve different characters, the reference to the matter in the book of Deuteronomy—which names Dathan and Abiram but not Korah, and mentions the earthquake but not the fire—constituted an embarrassing challenge to the integrity of the Priestly work. No other Deuteronomic reference to JE accounts so blatantly interferred with the redactional enterprise of the Priestly tradent. That tradent therefore took special pains to add to the Reubenite genealogy in the census document the identification, "These (*hû'*) are the Dathan and Abiram. . . who strove against Moses and Aaron in the company of Korah." This is in the same style as the Priestly tradent's notation which we have observed in Exod. 6:26, identifying Aaron and Moses, thus: "These (*hû'*) are the Aaron and Moses to whom YHWH said. . ." Again we have a glimpse of the editorial task of the Priestly tradent, attempting to soften as much as possible the conflicts which were the natural and necessary results of his unique enterprise.

The daughters of Zelophehad, Num. 27:1-11. It is difficult to determine the stage at which this text entered the Priestly work.

The appointment of Joshua, Num. 27:12-23. In this pericope, the commission of Joshua is associated with the announcement of the death of Moses. Noth has regarded the matter of Joshua as having been added secondarily to the announcement concerning Moses, this addition having been made at the time when the Priestly work was joined to the Deuteronomistic history.[159] This view derives from Noth's premise that the Priestly work had no interest in the conquest and settlement of the land[160] and that therefore references to these matters in the Priestly style must be secondary adjustments to the attachment of the Priestly work to the Deuteronomistic history. This need not be the case, however, in this pericope. We have seen the extent to which the Priestly accounts are alternative expressions of the corresponding accounts in the JE sources. The association of the announcement of Moses' death and the appointment of Joshua in this pericope is no more than the Priestly expression of the same association in the JE account which, as we have seen in Chapter I, is now embedded in the midst of Dtr[1] and Dtr[2] materials in Deuteronomy 31.[161]

---

[159] *Numbers*, pp. 9,213.

[160] *UGS*, pp. 191f.

[161] Deut 31:14f.,23. See above, pp. 13f. Noth regards these three verses as Dtr.

Alternative to JE, this Priestly composition was one of the received materials of the Exilic tradent.

Additional sacrificial law, Num. 28,29. Noth has argued that this corpus of sacrificial law must be a later composition than the Numbers 15 corpus because, in the sacrificial law of Numbers 15, the cereal and drink offerings have the character of innovation while here they are presupposed as an effective regulation. We have reckoned Num. 15:1-31 as the work of the Exilic tradent, and so, acknowledging Noth's argument, we must reckon Num. 28,29 either to the Priestly tradent himself—in which case he composed it as presupposing his own earlier sacrificial law—or possibly as a secondary addition to the completed Priestly work.

Statutes on annulling women's vows, Numbers 30. This account continues the matter of Baal-Peor, Phinehas, etc. (Numbers 25), which we have reckoned among the received texts of the Priestly tradent. The continued disdain for the Midianites in this account may again reflect antagonism toward the Mushites. Though the text here portrays Moses as acting with particular zeal against them (31:14-18), such a portrayal is not necessarily inconsistent with polemic. Further, the text twice refers to the Levites with regard to their assignment to the service of the Tabernacle in the wording of Num. 17,18, which we have also reckoned as pre-Exilic texts. Most interesting is the treatment of Balaam in the midst of the pericope on the defeat of the Midianites (31:8,16). It is no surprise that P does not reproduce a full version of the JE Balaam cycle. The latter is anecdotal, includes an appearance of an angel, and portrays a talking ass. Nonetheless, in the JE narrative the matter of Baal-Peor follows that of Balaam (see also the reference to Balaam at Peor in Num. 23:28), and Mowinckel has argued that the association of the two matters in P especially points to the acquaintance of the Priestly author(s) with JE tradition.[162] The treatment of Balaam in Num. 31:8,16, therefore, is a Priestly alternative to its JE equivalent, deleting the anecdote of Balaam's blessing, the angel, and the talking animal, while substituting Midian for Moab. The entire Priestly treatment of the Midianite apostasy, from Phinehas at Baal-Peor to the subsequent defeat of the

---

Even if we were to concur that they are Dtr[(1)] the Priestly text in Numbers would still properly be regarded as alternative to them.

[162] Mowinckel, *Erwägungen zur Pentateuch Quellenfrage*, pp. 33f.; cf. Noth, *Numbers*, p. 231.

Midianites, is a complex alternative to both the Balaam cycle and the account of the Moabite apostasy in JE tradition. The hand which authored this Priestly version of these matters could not have been the same hand which joined this version to the JE narratives which it was clearly designed to replace. As alternative to the JE texts rather than elaboration of them, this Priestly material must have been created prior to the Priestly tradent in Exile.

Tribal portions, Num. 32:2-15,17-38; 33:50-56; 34-36. As all of this concluding material of the Tetrateuch relates to matters of apportionment of the land subsequent to the conquest, Noth again has regarded it as secondary addition to the completed Priestly work, introduced at the time of the joining of the Priestly work to the Deuteronomistic history. We have several reasons to be hesitant before this analysis. First, Noth has, like Mowinckel, recognized the dependence of P upon JE sources. Neither Noth nor Mowinckel, nonetheless, has explained the nature of that dependence. If I am correct in the judgment that the relationship in question is, in the first stage of the Priestly work, one of Priestly alternative composition to JE and Deuteronomistic tradition, then we have every reason to expect that the JE and Deuteronomistic traditions of the apportionment of the land by Moses should have their counterpart among the Priestly materials, which extend to the death of Moses. Second, the promise of the possession of the land is a major element of the Priestly presentation of the Patriarchal covenant (Gen. 17:8; 28:4; 35:12; 48:4; Exod. 6:4); it is particularly juxtaposed to the tribal blessings in Gen. 48:3-6; 49. We may therefore reasonably state that the tribal apportionments at the conclusion of the book of Numbers fall within the original range of the Priestly writer(s)' concerns. Noth has argued that "P puts the promise of land alongside the promise of descendants. . . because in the ancient tradition these matters belonged closely together, although he himself had no intention of speaking further about the fulfillment of this promise. . ."[163] This claim that the Priestly writer's numerous references to the promise of the land all arose because that writer was concerned with the promise of descendants and the two "belonged closely together" is untenable, especially in light of the fact that the reference to this promise in Exod. 6:4 (which Noth himself cites) does not mention the promise of descendants at all. Third, we must be open to the possibility that the

---

[163] *HPT*, p. 234n.

association of the Priestly work with the book of Deuteronomy (and thus necessarily with the Deuteronomistic history as well) was not a secondary literary development, but rather that the Priestly tradent included Deuteronomy in his original work. There is no denying Noth's observation that there is no trace of Priestly handling in Deuteronomy, but this is to be expected. Deuteronomy, unlike JE, had been formally promulgated with royal and priestly sanction, had been read publicly, was to be copied by each king (Deut. 17:18), was intended to be a pedagogical text (6:7; 11:19), and probably still had a party of supporters among the Levites. All of these factors would have prevented the Priestly tradent from tampering with the Deuteronomic text, but at the same time they might well have made its inclusion in the Priestly work quite important, perhaps mandatory, for the successful promulgation of the final product as *Torah*. The Exilic tradent thus was free to rework the JE sources, but could do no more with Deuteronomy than to include it. Its special character, cast as a final speech of Moses in the Plains of Moab, rendered its inclusion in its entirety at the close of the Priestly work a relatively uncomplicated editorial task. Further, by the time of the composition of Ezra and Nehemiah at the latest, the Torah apparently included both the Priestly material and Deuteronomy. We have already noted the reference in Neh. 8:13-18 to the matter of booths on the Sukkot festival, recalling one of the latest passages in the Priestly work (Lev. 23:39-42). A reference to the Deuteronomic law that an Ammonite and a Moabite may not enter the congregation (Deut. 23:4-6) also appears in Neh. 13:1f.[164] There is therefore a substantial likelihood that the Priestly work included the book of Deuteronomy. In either case, there is no reason to challenge the originality of the Priestly materials which relate the apportionment of the land by Moses. The references to the two-and-a-half tribes who settle East of Jordan, to the command to drive out the inhabitants of the land, and to the establishment of cities of refuge all are Priestly texts which have counterparts in JE and Deuteronomistic

---

[164] J.M. Myers argues that the book which Ezra brought with him was substantially our present Pentateuch, *Ezra/Nehemiah, The Anchor Bible*, pp. LIX-LXII. Examination of the prayers of Nehemiah in Nehamiah 1 and 9 confirms the acquaintance of the author of these texts with JE, Priestly, and Deuteronomic materials. Deuteronomic references include Neh. 1:9, which is reminiscent of the language of Deut. 30:1-10 (Dtr²) while refering to the Name theology in the manner of Dtr¹; Neh. 9:21 may be compared to Deut. 8:4.

literature. The list of tribal leaders in Num. 34:19-28, Noth acknowledges, is an original list, i.e. it is another use of this received text by the Priestly tradent. These last chapters of the Priestly work in the book of Numbers therefore may be regarded as part of the original work, most probably from its first stage.[165]

The Stations list, Num. 33:1-49. This list, as Cross has demonstrated, is the received document from which the Exilic tradent constructed the framework from the wilderness materials.

The death of Moses, Deut. 32:48-52; 34:7-9. The divine command to Moses to ascend Abarim, 32:48-52 is an expanded repetition of the Priestly text of Num. 27:12-14. This second appearace of the command is the resumptive editorial device of the Exilic tradent. The report of the death of Moses in Deut. 34:7-9 is the Priestly version of the JE report which precedes it (34:1-6) and of the Deuteronomistic report which follows it (34:10-12).

In the light of the foregoing study of the Priestly portions of the Pentateuch, we may begin to form a picture of the nature of the task at each stage of the Priestly work. At the first stage of the work we have a collection of accounts, lists, and legal materials. They express, for the most part, Priestly (specifically Aaronid) alternatives to JE and Deuteronomistic compositions. They reflect a consistent perspective with regard to certain fundamental matters, namely: the absence of sacrifice prior to the inauguration of the Priesthood and Tabernacle, the limitation upon blatant anthropomorphism, the absence of angels and dreams, the three-stage development of the revelation of the divine name, the division of the Israelites into priests, Levites, and laymen with delineation of the prerogatives of each. This collection of Priestly compositions, further, is an incomplete corpus. Parts of accounts are missing, and matters which seem crucial to the Priestly perspective are not

---

[165] See also J. Blenkinsopp, "The Structure of P," *CBQ* 38 (1976), pp. 275-292, challenging Noth's view that P has no interest in conquest and occupation.

treated; and without the *tôlᵉdōt*, plagues, and Stations frameworks the whole does not hold together well. We do not know, therefore, in what form it existed prior to reaching the hands of the Exilic tradent. We do not know if any part of it was read publicly as the Deuteronomists' book was. We know that some portion of it was known and challenged by Jeremiah.

The second stage of the Priestly work is an Exilic product. Despite the fact that its tradent was heavily dependent upon his received texts for accounts, legislation, and framework materials, it was nonetheless his creativity which was responsible for the existence of the Torah, and it was his historical experience, namely Exile, which was the milieu out of which the Torah was born. Though he did not compose the sort of textual modifications which the editor of Dtr² did in Exile—i.e. additions to the received text, specifically designed to impose an Exilic perspective upon the whole—the Priestly tradent's impact upon his final product was no less creative and no less profound. He welded doublet and contradicting traditions into a single work which was sufficiently unified to be acceptable as the Torah for millennia. It is not J or P that humans have read for these millennia, after all, but the Torah, i.e. the work of the Priestly tradent in Exile.

II. The editorial work of the Exilic Priestly tradent.

Our first question concerning the work of the Exilic tradent is whether this unique enterprise produced a composition which was more than the sum of its parts. The pre-Exilic Priestly compositions had, after all, been composed as alternative Torah to the JE and Deuteronomic texts because of the Priestly writer(s)' apparent dissatisfaction with these texts. The combination of these Priestly compositions with the very texts to which they were alternative—and the promulgation of this combined product as "the Torah of Moses which YHWH God of Israel had given,"[166] —is one of the

---

[166] Ezra 7:6; Neh. 8:1.

most ironic examples of literary history of any work. The reason(s) for the combination of the two remains a mystery. It may owe to a compromise between factions who supported the legitimacy of each *tôrāh*. It may be that both *tôrôt* had become sufficiently well-known that exclusion of one or the other was not possible. I.e. the Aaronids could not successfully promulgate a *tôrāh* which did not include the familiar stories of Eden, Babel, Sodom (all JE); and a *tôrāh* which did not include the also-familiar stories of Moses' glowing face, Korah's rebellion, and Phinehas' zeal (all P) likewise could not be successfully promulgated. The alternative *tôrôt*, meanwhile, could not simply be arranged e.g., in the manner of the Gospels in the New Testament—i.e., side by side, each preserved complete—because the *tôrôt* were all attributed to the same author, Moses himself. Thus a complex design would be required in which alternative *tôrôt* could merge satisfactorily.

In order to measure the impact of the tradent who conceived and executed this design, one must determine whether this ironic combination of alternative *tôrôt* produced a portrayal of YHWH's relations with humans which differed in significant ways froms its components' respective portrayals. Martin Noth wrote that, precisely because P depended upon the JE sources (or because both depended upon a common *Grundlage*), the combination of P and JE did not result in any major new element, historical or theological, in the unified Priestly work.[167] The present analysis of the literary history of the Torah, however, leads one to perceive several significant metamorphoses in the conception of God and in the portrayal of the *magnalia Dei* which result from the Exilic tradent's design.

The juxtaposition of the JE and Priestly Creation accounts, first, precipitated a narrative synthesis with exegetical possibilities which neither of the original documents possessed independently. The humans who reach to the Tree of Knowledge of Good and Evil are different from all other creatures in that they bear the stamp of the *imago Dei*. Without pursuing the precise meaning of *sélem* and *dᵉmût*, one can say at minimum that humans are portrayed as

---

[167] "Partly in consequence of a common harking back to a fully developed oral narrative tradition, and partly in consequence of mutual literary dependence, the course of history was narrated so much the same in all the sources that even their combination with one another could change nothing essential in this regard." Noth, *HPT*, p. 250.

embodying some divine element—and this element is critical to the events of Eden. Insofar as beings who share some quality with YHWH are nonetheless treated by him as his subordinates, his communication with them being initially and nearly exclusively commands, the stage is set for their disobedience even before the introduction of the serpent as catalyst. When Mark Twain queried, "If the Lord didn't want humans to be rebellious, then why did he create them in his image?" he was at his incisive and theologically ironic best. Depicted as creating humans in his own image and then setting under prohibition the fruit whose very attraction is to endow one with a divine power, YHWH is thus portrayed as himself creating the terms of that tension which results in human disobedience. Themselves possessing some godly quality, the humans are attracted precisely by the serpent's claim that if they eat from the tree they will be like God(s). This tension, however, is neither the work of the author of J nor the work of the pre-Exilic Priestly author. It is purely a by-product of the combination of the two at the hand of the Exilic tradent. P does not portray a primal human rebellion; J does not portray the creation of humans in the image of God. The combination of these two re-cast the motive of the human's actions in Eden. In the final product which we call Torah, one cannot separate the creation *in imago Dei* from the natures of the humans who disobey the divine instruction. Interestingly, Noth referred to this identification of the humans who are created in the divine image with the humans who rebel, but he concluded only that the combined text thus accurately reflects a condition of humankind, while he held nonetheless that this effect of combination of texts still constitutes no new narrative or theological component of the whole.[168] In response, I would insist that the effect of the combination of these originally alternative texts was profound—in this case refocusing the perspective of the first chapters of the Biblical narrative. Indeed, insofar as the struggle between YHWH and the human community persists as an obvious and dominant theme in Biblical narrative, the Gen. 1-3 account of the archetype of that struggle sets a fundamental *Leitmotif* of those narratives. From this perspective, it is difficult to overestimate the impact of the tradent who produced in Gen. 1-3 a narrative which is quite literally more than the sum of its components.

---

[168] *HPT*, p. 251.

One may observe a broader metamorphosis in the portrayal of YHWH in the unified Priestly work when one compares certain features of the JE and Priestly theologies. It is regularly noted in theological studies of the Hebrew Bible that one finds in P a more cosmic perspective of YHWH than in the JE narratives.[169] Specifically, one observes, first, that the Sabbath is fixed in the orders of Creation in P, while it is not in J, and functions as commemorative of historical national events in D. Second, the Priestly Creation account depicts the construction of the entire universe, describing the "cosmic bubble" as discussed above,[170] while the J Creation focuses exclusively on the earth and the birth of plant and animal life thereon, with YHWH personally moving about among his creatures. Interestingly, the Priestly narrative begins: "When God began to create *the heavens and the earth*," (Gen. 1:1) while J begins: "In the day that YHWH God made *earth and heaven*," (2:4b). The reversed order, as it happens, is appropriate to the respective points of view.[171] Again in the Flood account, also noted above,[172] P portrays a cosmic crisis in which the habitable bubble is threatened, while the J version merely reports rain. P, further, adds the Noahic covenant to those of JE tradition (the Abrahamic and Israelite covenants), thus setting the latter covenants, which bind YHWH to a particular community of humans, into a larger framework of a covenant with all flesh. In all of these instances the Priestly writer portrays YHWH in conceptually broader terms than those of the JE portrayal. As discussed above, the pre-Exilic Priestly compositions consistently desist from the angelic and blatantly anthropomorphic portrayals which are widespread in JE tradition. It is no oversimplification to characterize P as a more clearly cosmic portrayal of the deity, and JE as a more personal conception. But, again, the merging of the two portrayals in the unified work of the Exilic Priestly tradent yielded a new formula, i.e. a synthesis in which the cosmic and the personal aspects of God stood in a balance which was unlike that of either of the component compositions. It is this theological synthesis, in which YHWH appears as both universal and personal, as both the

---

[169] E.g. von Rad, *Old Testament Theology*, I pp. 148f.; E. A. Speiser, *Genesis* pp. XXVff.

[170] See above, p. 82.

[171] See Speiser, *Genesis*, pp. 18f.

[172] P. 82, n. 94.

Creator and "the God of your father," that has seeded Jewish and Christian conceptions of God for millennia. Yet it was neither the conception of JE nor of P—but rather something new, a product of the union of the two at the hand of the Exilic tradent.

A second synthetic theological formulation was born in the unified Priestly work with regard to the portrayal of the mercy of YHWH. The centrality of the mercy of YHWH to JE tradition is manifest in the divine formula which is revealed to Moses on Sinai in Exod. 34:6f. YHWH is "merciful and gracious, long-forbearing and abundant in ḥesed. . ." It is upon this formula that Moses bases his appeal that YHWH rescind his condemnation of the nation following the spy incident (Num. 14:13-20). The appeal is successful, as was Moses' prior appeal following a similar condemnation in the golden calf incident (Exod. 32:11-14). Israel's God, in JE portrayal, is a deity who can be "grieved to his heart" by the actions of his humans (Gen. 6:6). The well-known compassion of YHWH, which is responsible for innumerable reprieves for Israel's continual violations of covenant in JE and Deuteronomistic literature—and which pervade the Psalms and Prophetic literature—is, however, almost entirely unknown in P. The fundamental vocabulary of the category of mercy, formalized in the divine formula of Exodus 34, is completely missing in the pre-Exilic Priestly compositions. All forms of the root *rḥm* are missing, as are all forms of *ḥnn*.[173] There is not a single reference to the *ḥesed* of YHWH.[174] The regular Biblical term for repentance, *šwb*, never appears in P.[175] Not only is the terminology of divine mercy absent in P, but the portrayal of it as a phenomenon in narrative is exceedingly rare as well. Notably, Moses' appeal for mercy in the matter of the spies in JE is simply eliminated in the Priestly version of that episode. In P, instead of YHWH's sentence being made more lenient as a result of the arguments of Moses, the sentence is simply pronounced and carried out. The similar appeal of Moses in JE in the matter of the golden calf of course has no counterpart in P. This absence of concern

---

[173] The second element of the threefold Priestly blessing (Num. 6:25) is the lone possible exception to the absence of the root *ḥnn*, but, as noted above, this passage may be Exilic.

[174] The mention of *ḥesed* in the Decalogue is common to the Exodus 20 and Deuteronomy 5 versions and is clearly related to the Exodus 34 formula. It is therefore not original to P.

[175] See Milgrom, *Cult and Conscience*, pp. 121ff.

with mercy, grace, *ḥesed*, and repentance in P is itself a valuable datum for exegesis, and for dating as well.[176] My present concern, however, is specifically to note the effect of the combination of the differing compositions. Quite simply, the uniting of the JE and Priestly texts within the single Priestly work resulted in a new theological formula of justice and mercy which corresponded neither to that of JE nor to that of P. The proportional ratio of these qualities to one another within the character of YHWH in the Priestly work bore no resemblance to that of either of its components. The portrayal of YHWH in the united Torah therefore depicts the deity as embodying a quality of compassion which the pre-Exilic Priestly writer(s) never intended to emphasize so, while it develops the reverse constituent of the divine character far beyond the original portrayal thereof in JE texts. A new view of the tension between the divine traits of mercy and justice was thus born in the design of the Exilic tradent.

In a still more pervasive synthesis, the design of the Priestly tradent in Exile resulted in a portrayal of the relations of YHWH and humans in which a distinct shift in the humans' share of control of events becomes apparent in the course of the narrative. To analyse this effect of the Exilic tradent's work, it is necessary, first, to observe the shape of this phenomenon in the JE narrative.

The JE Creation account portrays YHWH and humans in a state of intimacy which is without parallel in any Biblical material following the expulsion from Eden. Yahweh fashions the man and woman himself, breathes life into the man's nostrils, plants the garden, forms animals for the man's sake, walks in the garden, speaks directly to the humans, feeds them, orders them, chastises them, makes their clothes. YHWH's dealings with their descendant Noah require of the latter a level of responsibility not expected of the first man and woman. But for the notation that YHWH himself shuts Noah in the ark (Gen. 7:16b), the text portrays YHWH as giving instructions and Noah as executing the required actions. YHWH clothes Adam, but Noah has to build the ark himself. Himself responsible for his survival, his personality more explicitly drawn than that of Adam or Cain, Noah is more a *Mensch* than Adam.

---

[176] If P were Exilic, the absence of any reference to repentence or to divine mercy would be strange indeed.

The participation and responsibility of humans in events, natural and miraculous, continues to develop in this direction through the patriarchal narratives. Even YHWH's shutting of the ark has no parallel in the JE patriarchal materials for direct divine tending. Abraham is still more a *Mensch* than his predecessors. The Abrahamic accounts are more personal and less archetypal than those which precede; and the demands upon Abraham's own energy, from the first *lek l^ekā* to the test on Moriah, far exceed those of prior narrative. The text is replete with appearances of YHWH and his angels and perhaps even a divine appearance in human form,[177] but even in this state of considerable contact with the divine presence there is not the hand which made Adam's and Eve's loincloths and shut Noah's ark. There is rather the God who, before acting against Sodom, asks, "Shall I hide from Abraham that which I am doing?" (Gen. 18:17). Abraham is not only informed of a divine intention, he has even an opportunity to challenge it, albeit exceedingly humbly and via a series of questions rather than declarative arguments (vv. 23-33). Another dimension is thus ceded to the human role in divine/human relations. This growing participation of humans is further apparent in Lot's successfully persuading YHWH not to destroy Zoar so that he might seek refuge there (Gen. 19:17-21), to which YHWH responds, "Escape there quickly, because I cannot do a thing until you arrive there," (v. 22). Embedded in these J accounts is a narrowing apparent divine control of events, coupled with an inverse increase in the human share.

As the JE narrative unfolds, nearly every unit adds a level of this phenomenon to what precedes it. The account of Abraham's servant and Rebekah portrays the servant as himself determining

---

[177] The form of YHWH's appearance in Genesis 18 is a subject of disagreement. The case for the understanding that one of the three visitors is YHWH, the others angels, is based on the following: (1) There seems to be no demonstrable gap between v. 1 and v. 2, so that v. 2 appears to begin an account of the appearance announced in v. 1. (2) Abraham, prostrating himself before the three *'ănāšîm*, speaks to only one of them, as indicated by the singular pronominal suffix of *b^eênêkā* (v. 3), and addresses him as *'ădōnāy*. The MT pointing with a *qames* in the final syllable is the form of the divine title *Lord* (LXX: κυριε, Targum: *ywy.* (3) The text alternates thereafter, first portraying all three visitors as speaking (v. 9), then an unnamed one of the three (v. 10) speaks, then YHWH himself speaks words which identify him with the unnamed one (v. 14). (4) We are told in v. 22 that the following chapter begins (19:1), "And the *two* angels came to Sodom."

the sign by which YHWH points to the right woman (Gen. 24:12). In the Jacob/Esau materials, the birthright and the blessings of YHWH can be manipulated and redirected by the guile of a man (Gen. 25:29-34; 27). In YHWH's last appearance in human form, Jacob struggles with him, prevails, and *demands* blessing (Gen. 32:22-33). In the Joseph account we find the beginnings of the attitude toward YHWH which develops strongly in the Deuteronomistic material, as we have seen in Chapter I; namely, YHWH is portrayed as working behind the scenes in undefined ways (cf. Gen. 39:2f.,21,23) and endowing a man with a special ability which is the medium of his and his family's preservation. The E account especially develops this approach in the conversations of Joseph with Pharaoh and with the brothers (Gen. 41:16,25,28,32,39; 45:5b-9). We may also note again the growing centrality of the human figures through the Jacob and Joseph materials which, in terms of development of character, surpasses all preceding personalities. Nor can this phenomenon be explained merely in terms of the larger body of material in the latter cases. The difference is not only quantitative. The nature of the Jacob/Esau/Laban/Joseph materials is simply more communicative of the personalities of each of these four than are the accounts of Adam, Cain, Noah, Abraham, or Isaac. The figures become more identifiable personalities in parallel development with the phenomenon of their broadening status in relation to YHWH. The portrayal of Jacob presents a more complex character than those of his father and grandfather; the man whose dominant trait is guile in the first units of the narrative changes into another sort of man in the later units—and the turning point is precisely his face-to-face struggle with YHWH. This episode is set at the juncture between the end of the Laban cycle and the beginning of the Joseph cycle. It is at this juncture that Jacob ceases to be cast as the sly deceiver. We observe Jacob's growing and maturing, and we observe that of Joseph as well. Joseph grows from the youth who offends brothers and father with his recounting of his self-focused dreams into the man who minimizes his brothers' feelings of guilt by declaring to them that their ill-intended actions were in fact divinely guided toward survival of the family. This maturing in Joseph, too, takes place in parallel with his acquisition of that which he understands to be a power of divine origin. He graduates from being a lad who does not apparently perceive the impact of his own dreams, arriving at a level at which he wields the power to interpret the dreams of Pharaoh. As the JE narrative proceeds, the humans thus become more identifiable and more significant *as individuals*; and these individuals exercise more apparent control over the events in which they figure.

The entrance of Moses in the JE narrative marks the beginning of yet another stage in the growing participation of humans in the events of the Biblical history, and a new stage in development of character as well. From Moses' first encounter with YHWH at the burning bush, through the ordeals of Egypt and wilderness, his own character, his strengths and occasionally his weaknesses, are a governing force in the events to an extent unmatched by any previous figure. Though it is YHWH who chooses and directs Moses, despite the man's own reluctance, Moses' personal role in all that proceeds is so central as to make him appear to be a god himself (Exod. 4:16-J). Nearly all of the miraculous events which follow, though proceeding from YHWH's power, are announced, initiated, and concluded by the word or action of Moses. While some of the plagues upon Egypt, for example, are described by the JE narrators as YHWH's own doing (Exod. 9:15,18), more often the timing of the onset and the conclusion of the plagues is attached to the figure of Moses (Exod. 8:27; 9:22,33; 10:12,18,21f). Moses insists that YHWH directs his actions, as is especially clear in his response to the challenge of Dathan and Abiram: ". . . YHWH has sent me to do all these things, not from my own heart," (Num. 16:28). But the very fact that Moses must say this underscores the portrayal of the impression which the man Moses himself makes upon his contemporaries.

The portrayal of the manner in which Moses speaks to YHWH, as well, indicates the point to which human stance has developed in relation to YHWH. Especially enlightening and moving are Moses' words of complaint (Num. 11:11-15):

Why have you done harm to your servant and why have I not found favor in your sight that you lay the burden of this whole people on me. Did I conceive this whole people, did I give birth to it, that you say to me: carry it in your bosom as the nurse carries the suckling to the land which you swore to its fathers. I am not able, I myself, to bear this whole people, for it is too heavy for me. And if you do thus to me, kill me please if I have found favor in your eyes, and let me not see my wretchedness.

As much as Abraham's plea in the matter of Sodom (Genesis 18) impressed us as a stage in *Menschlichkeit* and in growth of the human role in the JE narrative, that confrontation is nevertheless not the equal of this awesome moment of Moses' anguished words. Abraham's humbly-phrased questions in Genesis 18 contrast sharply with Moses' outright protest. Moses' appeals in the incidents of the golden calf and of the spies, discussed above, likewise betray a change in the focus upon human community relative to the appeal of Abraham, moving from Abraham's argument, which is an appeal to YHWH's own standard, viz. "Will the judge of all the earth not do justly?" to Moses' appeals, each of which seeks to persuade the deity on grounds of what the *human* kingdoms will say about him, thus:

> Why should the Egyptians say: He brought them out for evil, to kill them in the mountains and to consume them from the face of the earth?

> Exod. 32:12

> . . . and the nations which have heard about you will say: Because YHWH was not able to bring this people to the land which he swore to them, he slaughtered them in the wilderness.

> Num. 14:15b, 16

To emphasize the inverse nature of the developing divine/human equation, we should note that alongside the phenomenon of the growing human base in the Biblical narrative stands the phenomenon of changing manifestations of the deity. While we could not deny the importance of theophany in the JE picture of the Mosaic age, we nevertheless perceive that a level of immanence has been lost relative to the primeval history and the patriarchal narratives. In the Mosaic narrative, YHWH goes among (*bqrb*) Israel, he is with (*ʿm*) them, he appears in a column of cloud and fire. But these portrayals do not convey the immediacy of YHWH which is primary in the accounts of Adam and Cain. Even Moses' encounter with YHWH at the burning bush has not the closeness of Jacob's and Abraham's encounters with YHWH in actual contact with some human form. The critical exception in this development is the experience of Moses which is told in Exodus 33 and 34. This is the ultimate experience of YHWH, not capable of comparison with any other for immediacy or intensity, standing as a unique and consummate moment. But this scene itself reflects a transition into *mediated* divine/human encounter, in which the role of the prophet as a human medium of divine communication is critical. Whereas YHWH himself pronounces the Decalogue in the presence of the entire people of Israel initially, the people themselves call upon Moses to act as go-between. All communication is channelled through Moses thereafter. YHWH himself inscribes the Decalogue, and Moses carries the tablets to the community. Miriam, Aaron, and seventy elders also function as prophetic channels of the divine communication, but this too produces a significant development in the changing manifestations of the deity among humans. When Aaron and Miriam challenge Moses with the argument that YHWH has spoken through them as well, YHWH declares:

> If there will be a prophet among you
> I YHWH shall make myself known to him
>   in a vision,
> in a dream I shall speak in him;
> not so my servant Moses -
> in all my house he is faithful -
> mouth to mouth I shall speak in him
> and by vision, and not by enigmas
> and he will see the form of YHWH.

Num. 12:6-8

It is thus understood in JE tradition that Moses knew a direct experience of YHWH which no contemporary or successor equalled. Prophecy after Moses is restricted to dream and vision.

One may perceive in this sequence a transition in the balance of the divine/human equation, in which the narrative focus increasingly draws us to the human characters and in which these humans themselves increasingly control both natural and supernatural power over the events of their lives. The combination of the JE narratives with the Priestly accounts sharpened this transition at several narrative junctures. Thus in the Priestly version of the Abrahamic covenant Abraham doubts the divine promise of the birth of Isaac, and he urges rather that *'ēl šadday* accept Ishmael. His request is denied, however, and the decision regarding the bearer of the patriarchal succession remains the prerogative of the deity. When the Priestly and JE texts were combined, this Priestly account of the designation of Isaac as prime heir came to stand in contrast with the JE account of the designation of Jacob. In that JE account, as noted above, the cunning of Rebekah and Jacob is responsible for the course of events.[178] The Isaac/Jacob text of course necessarily followed the Abraham/Isaac material chronologically, and, thus juxtaposed, the two stories contribute to the impression of increasing human control of events.

The presence of both the E and the Priestly versions of the Meribah episode in the tradent's arrangement likewise contributes to the impression of a gradually shifting control. The E version is set shortly following the exodus (Exod. 17:2-7) and portrays Moses as simply obeying the orders of YHWH to strike the rock which is to yield water, while YHWH stands upon the rock before him. The Priestly version (Num. 20:2-13) now appears as a subsequent event, in which Moses blatantly disobeys the divine instruction to speak to the rock in the sight of the congregation. Though Moses does not speak to the rock but rather strikes it, the miracle occurs nevertheless. Such power to alter a miracle is unknown in Biblical narrative prior to Moses. The divine response which follows, perhaps the most severe sentence which could possibly be imposed upon Moses, only sharpens our awareness of the magnitude of what Moses had done—but, though he suffers this heartrending divine reprimand and chastisement for his action, the fact remains that he was able to perform it. The united Priestly and JE text further sharpened the impression of the growth of the human role in great events in other Mosaic narratives. As in JE, the Priestly writer noted that Moses, himself participating in the control of power, seems to men to be a god (Exod. 7:1). Though YHWH is master of the events of the exodus, Moses' part is crucial. Thus YHWH declares, "*I* shall bring my signs and wonders. . .*I* shall lay my hand on Egypt. . .*I* shall stretch out my hand on Egypt. . . *I* shall bring out my people," (Exodus 7), but the text nevertheless portrays the plagues which follow as occurring at the initiation of Moses and Aaron. So great is the role of Moses and Aaron in the exodus and Wilderness events that, in the portrayal of the first murmuring episode, it is necessary for Moses to tell the people, "Your murmurings are not against us (Moses and Aaron) but against YHWH," (Exod. 16:8; see also Num. 16:11 - P). This Priestly text complemented the JE dialogue of Moses and Dathan/Abiram, discussed above, underscoring the portrayal of the impression which Moses'

---

[178] The prediction of this outcome in Gen. 25:23 does not lead us necessarily to see divine predestination, but only pre-cognition, in this episode.

own use of power makes upon his community.

The combination of JE and Priestly texts further strengthened the portrayal of Moses' mediating role in divine/human communication through the juxtaposition of the respective accounts of Moses' experience on Sinai. As noted above, the JE texts depict the ultimate revelation which Moses experiences (Exodus 34); the description of Moses' subsequent descent from the mount is Priestly. In this latter description Aaron and the people see the glowing skin of Moses' face and fearfully perceive his singular role.

We have observed here several cases in which the web of JE and Priestly texts enhanced the original JE impression of gradual transition in the human share of the responsibility for their experience, as well as two cases in which the combinatory design itself resulted in stages of this transition which were native to neither of the component texts. The covenant sequence in the pre-Exilic Priestly texts further enhanced this impression. First, the signs of the three covenants suggested this transition. Elohim sets the bow in the heavens as sign of the first covenant. The sign of the Abrahamic covenant, circumcision, is the responsibility of the human recipients of the covenant themselves. In the Israelite covenant, the observance of the Sabbath as covenant sign entails fulfilling a lifelong obligation involving a variety of responsibilities. Each successive covenant presumes a larger contribution from the human partners. Indeed, the first two covenants are divine bestowals upon meritorious figures while the third is a covenant of obligation, making considerable future demands upon the energy of the recipients. The Noahic covenant is eternal and unconditional, requiring nothing of the recipients (all flesh) for its preservation. The Abrahamic covenant is bestowed with only one demand, namely the execution of the covenant sign. The Israelite covenant, however, is a structure of stipulations, from the primary commands of the Decalogue to the details of Tabernacle, purity, sacrifice, etc.[179] When the Exilic tradent combined the JE and Priestly texts, this Priestly covenant framework further enhanced the impression in the Torah narrative that a shift occurs in the apparent human share of responsibility for the course of their relations with YHWH.

---

[179] Cf. D.N. Freedman, "Divine Commitment and Human Obligation," *Interpretation* 18 (1964), pp. 419-431; Weinfeld, "The Covenant of Grant in the Old Testament and in the Ancient Near East," *JAOS* 90 (1970), pp. 184-203.

The enterprise of the Priestly tradent thus resulted in a Torah whose theology was neither independent of its sources nor a simple composite of them. That tradent effected a metamorphosis in the representation of the character of YHWH and of the course of his relations with humans. The manner in which this new representation in the Priestly work linked with the corresponding matters in the work of the Exilic Deuteronomist (Dtr[2]) is the subject of my concluding observations.

Conclusion

The Final Product

Once the book of Deuteronomy came to be joined to the Tetrateuch—whether in the Exilic tradent's design or in a subsequent operation—the association of the Torah with the Deuteronomistic history as a continuing account was natural. Several factors rendered this a comfortable union. First, the book of Deuteronomy was an ideal pivot for the two works. As we have seen in Chapter II, Deuteronomy frequently presumes or quotes the JE accounts (above p. 121). It also shares several common expressions with P (pp. 107ff.) and, in its final form, contains the expanded repetition of the Priestly account of Moses' ascent of Abarim (p. 191f). At the same time that Deuteronomy thus looks back to JEP, it looks forward into the Deuteronomistic history as well, owing to the constructions of both Dtr^1 and Dtr^2, as we have seen in Chapter I. Thus the book of Deuteronomy, structurally, provided a suitable linkage of the Priestly work and the Deuteronomistic history. Second, the presence of Patriarchal and Mosaic covenant traditions in the course of the Deuteronomistic history enhanced the bond between that history and the Torah, which portrays the establishment of the covenants.

Third, we observed in Chapter I the vacillating balance between the anger and the mercy of YHWH in Dtr^1. The presence of this balance in Dtr^1, we noted, made possible the reversals of perspective which the Exilic Deuteronomist constructed, turning the emphasis from the threats of *'ēl qannā'* to the compassion of *'ēl raḥûm* (pp. 69ff.). We then observed, in Chapter II, the development of the particular tension between the divine traits of mercy and justice which resulted from the union of JE and Priestly compositions in the Priestly work (pp. 199ff.). When Torah and Deuteronomistic history became associated, the presence of this tension in the Priestly work was manifestly suitable to the complete Dtr^2 portrayal of the course of the history of Israel subsequent to Moses in this regard.

Perhaps the most interesting bond in the union of the Exilic Deuteronomistic and Priestly works is in the realm of the progressive shift in the divine/human balance of control of events. We have observed, in Chapter II, the extent to which this phenomenon developed in the combination of JE and Priestly narratives in the Priestly work. There the growth of the human role in the use of power culminates in the figure of Moses. This development continues naturally in the Deuteronomistic history. As noted at the outset of the discussion in Chapter I of the control of miracle in the Deuteronomistic history, the role attributed to Joshua in the miraculous halting of the sun exceeds the degree to which even Moses is portrayed as participating in the choice and timing of miracles, and the human control of miracle continues to grow thereafter (pp. 64f.). We observed there that this qualitative change in the portrayal of miraculous events contributes to an image of a diminishing apparent presence of YHWH in human affairs. With the union of Torah and $n^e b\hat{i}^v\hat{i}m$ $r\bar{i}^{v}\check{s}\bar{o}n\hat{i}m$, that image was complete, extending from YHWH's manifest control of miraculous activity in Genesis and Exodus to the personal miracles of Elijah, Elisha, and Isaiah in the books of Kings. We observed that quantitatively, as well, the treatment of miracle in the Deuteronomistic history suggests the diminishing apparent presence of YHWH, the portrayal of public miracle ending abruptly following the account of Elijah on Carmel. In this respect, also, the association of the Priestly work and the Deuteronomistic history enhanced this notion of diminishing divine immanence, for the combination of JE and Priestly versions of miraculous events simply increased the total number of such events in the completed Priestly work, yielding a greater number of plagues in Egypt, two extractions of water from rocks, both earthquake and fire in the Dathan/Abiram/Korah incident, etc. The more signs and wonders thus ascribed to the Patriarchal and Mosaic periods, the more striking was the subsequent diminution and ultimate disappearance of these events in the Deuteronomistic history.

The framework which the Exilic Priestly tradent had constructed in order to house these JE and Priestly accounts of the plagues further enhanced this development. In the JE account, Pharaoh repeatedly hardens his heart (Exod. 8:11,28; 9:7,34; 10:1), himself electing to resist the power of YHWH. In the Priestly version, it is YHWH who hardens Pharaoh's heart (7:3,13,22; 8:15; 9:12,35). The Exilic tradent based his unifying framework upon the Priestly model, thus inserting into the JE text of YHWH's instructions to Moses the announcement that YHWH will harden Pharaoh's heart (4:21b), inserting fulfillment notices of this action at the end of JE plague accounts (9:35; 10:20,27), and inserting a summary which repeated this fact (11:10). Thus constructed, the final unified version of the plagues eliminated the original JE perspective of the plagues as the defeat of a man by a God. The JE notations that Pharaoh hardened his heart now appeared merely as YHWH's execution of his stated intention. In this final version, YHWH controls both sides of the dynamic, toying with Pharaoh's will in order that "Egypt will know that I am YHWH when I stretch forth my hand upon Egypt," (7:5). This magnified depiction of the dimensions of YHWH's power in the generation of Moses further sharpened the image of a diminishing apparent involvement of YHWH in the Deuteronomistic narratives of the events of subsequent ages.

As the combinatory design of the Exilic tradent produced the appearance of a greater abundance of miracles in the early ages than any of the component traditions had suggested, so a similar development occurred in that tradent's work with regard to the portrayal of theophanies in those ages. YHWH was now portrayed as appearing to Abraham both on those occasions which the JE narrative had depicted and on those which the pre-Exilic Priestly writer(s) had intended as alternatives to those JE portrayals. Genesis 17 was no longer the Priestly depiction of the deity's self-introduction to Abraham, but was now only one of a series of the patriarch's encounters with his God. Gen. 35:9-15 was no longer a Priestly alternative to the E account of the naming of Bethel and to the J account of the change of Jacob's name at Penuel; rather, the combined text now portrayed what readers could only understand as an additional theophany in the course of Jacob's return. Exodus 6, likewise, originally a pre-Exilic Priestly alternative to the JE portrayals of YHWH's self-introduction to Moses in Midian, became instead a portrayal of the delivery of an additional set of divine instructions to Moses *following* his first meeting with Pharaoh. In each of these examples, as alternatives were transformed into doublets, the total effect in the combined text was to portray the deity as making himself known to humans more frequently in the Patriarchal and Mosaic eras than the authors of the component texts had intended. Since the editorial process which produced the Deuteronomistic history was manifestly different, as described in Chapter I, the examples of this combinatory multiplication of theophanies therein are fewer than in the Priestly work. The association of the Priestly work with the Deuteronomistic history, therefore; bolstered the impression of the diminishing apparent immanence of YHWH in human intercourse. As we observed in Chapter I, the portrayal of the appearances of YHWH, as expressed in the terms of *nr'h* and *nglh*, finally ceases altogether in the Deuteronomistic history following the reign of Solomon. The abundance of references to the $k^e b \hat{o} d$ *YHWH* and to the accompanying $^c \bar{a} n \bar{a} n$ in Priestly narrative likewise joined to a cessation of their portrayal in the course of the Deuteronomistic history. Again, as observed in Chapter I, the last reference to the appearance of the *kābôd* and *ʿānān* occurs in the account of the Temple dedication in the reign of Solomon.

As these marks of the divine presence in Israel which are widespread in the Priestly work make their successive exits from the Deuteronomistic history, the single channel which persists is the "Name theology." Its demise, as we have seen, occurs with the destruction of the Temple, as recounted in Dtr^2 (2 Kings 23:27). But the destruction of the Temple of Solomon does not mean only the elimination of the Deuteronomistic Name theology, but the elimination of the Priestly correspondent to the Name theology, namely the Tabernacle, as well. The Tabernacle and the Name theology are both tied to the Temple in 1 Kings 8. The ark and Tabernacle are brought to the Temple in conjunction with the consecration of that building as the place where YHWH's name will be. The attachment of the name to that place is referred to nine times in the portrayal of that ceremony (1 Kings 8:16-20,29,43,44,48). The fall of the Temple therefore cuts off the fundamental expressions of the presence of YHWH of both the Deuteronomistic and the Priestly theologies. The association of the Priestly work with the Deuteronomistic history thus again dramatises the notion of the receding immanence of the deity, in this instance through the complex editorial relationship of P, Dtr^1, and Dtr^2. Indeed, within this final arrangement of the materials, one can also trace a development from the Priestly portrayal of the revelation of the divine name (in the stages: Elohim, *ʾēl šadday*, YHWH), through the Dtr^1 attachment of that name to the chosen place as divine/human channel, to the Dtr^2 divine rejection of the channel. Thus even the Priestly depiction of an increasing particularity of the divine fell into place within an overall picture of decreasing communication with the deity. In this instance, as in the case of the terminology of theophany and in the portrayal of miracle, the association of the Priestly work with the Deuteronomistic history resulted ultimately in a portrayal of the diminishing immanence of YHWH in human affairs. From Genesis to Kings, YHWH had become a hidden God.

137

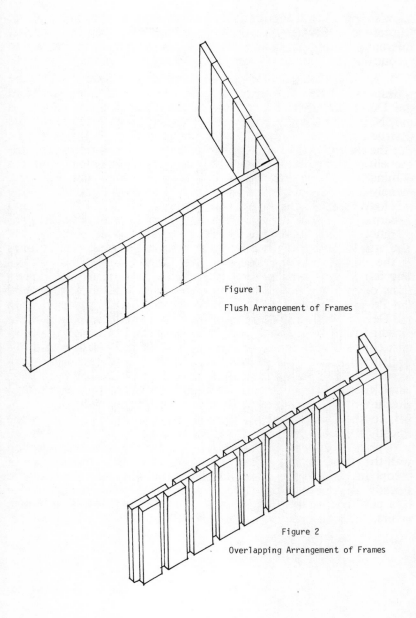

Figure 1

Flush Arrangement of Frames

Figure 2

Overlapping Arrangement of Frames

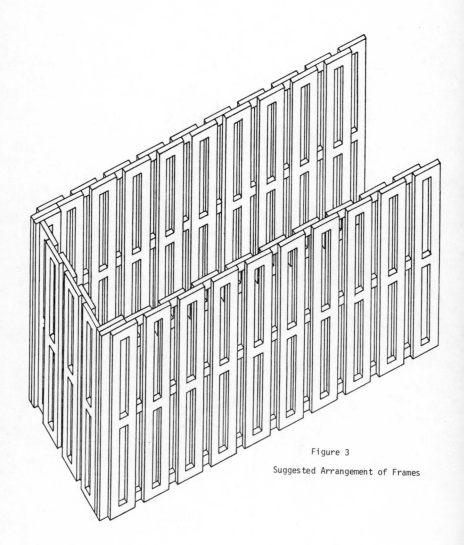

Figure 3

Suggested Arrangement of Frames

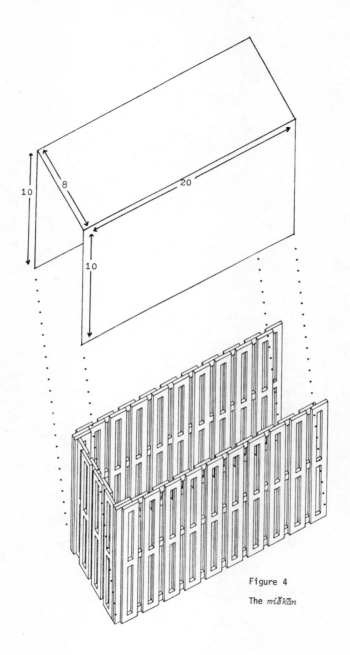

Figure 4

The *mi škān*

140

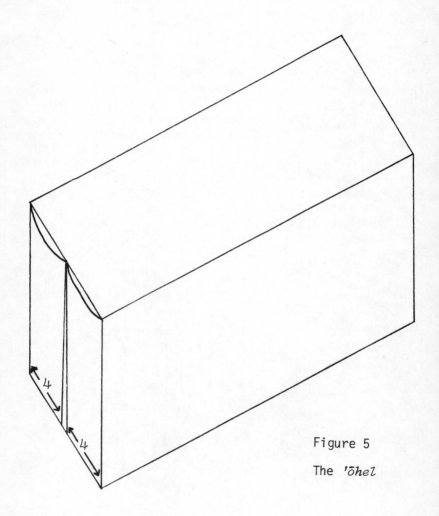

Figure 5

The *'ōhel*

Appendix: Verse Summary of Priestly Texts

Symbols: Pre-Exilic texts are identified with P^1,
Exilic texts are identified as P^2

The Book of Genesis

The Creation P^1
     1:2-2:3

tôl^{e}dōt (of) heaven and earth P^2
     2:4a

tôl^{e}dōt 'adam,   the *tôl^{e}dōt* book
     5:1-28, 30-32

The Flood P^1
     6:9-22; 7:11, 13-16a,24;
     8:1,2a,3b,4,5,7,13a,14-19;
     9:1-17

The years of Noah,   the *tôl^{e}dōt* book
     7:6; 9:28f.

tôl^{e}dōt (of) the sons of Noah, P^1 (10:1a,P^2)
     10:1-7,20,22,23,31,32

tôl^{e}dōt (of) Shem   the *tôl^{e}dōt* book
     11:10-26,32   (rubric, P^2)

The migration of Terah and Abraham P^1 (rubric, P^2)
     11:27,31; 12:4b,5

Lot P^1
     13:6,11b,12a; 19:29

Hagar and Ishmael P^1
     16:1a,3,15,16

Abrahamic covenant P^1
     17

142

The birth of Isaac 21:1b,2b-5	P[1]
The purchase of Machpelah 23	P[1]
The death of Abraham 25:7-11a	P[2]
tôlᵉdōt (of) Ishmael 25:12-17	P[1] (rubric, P[2])
tôlᵉdōt (of) Isaac 25:19	P[2]
Isaac marries Rebekah 25:20	P[1]
The wives of Esau 26:34f; 27:46; 28:1-9	P[1]
Jacob in Paddan-Aram 31:18b; 33:18b	P[2]
Jacob named Israel at Bethel 35:9-15	P[1]($^{c}ôd$, v.9, P[2])
Jacob's progeny 35:23-26	P[1]
Jacob's return to Isaac 35:27	?
The death of Isaac 35:28 35:29	P[1] P[2]
tôlᵉdōt (of) Esau 36	P[1] (rubric, P[2])
tôlᵉdōt (of) Jacob 37:2a	P[2]
Jacob and Joseph 37:1; 41:45b,46a; 46:6,7; 47:27b	P[1]

The Book of Exodus

144

145

The Book of Leviticus

Sacrificial law — P^1
  1-7:34,37f.

Anointing of Aaron — P^2
  7:35f.

The investment of Aaron — P^1
  8,9

The death of Nadab and Abihu, — P^1
  the charge to Aaron and his sons
  10

Law of clean and unclean — P^1
  11-15

Ritual of the Day of Atonement — P^1
  16

The Holiness Code — P^1
  17-26
  (Booths on Sukkot, 23:39-42) — P^2
  (Restoration from Exile, 26:39-45) — P^2

Appendix on dedicatory gifts — ?
  27

The Book of Numbers

Census — P^1 (1:1-4, P^2)
  1

Arrangement of the Camp — P^1
tôl^{e}dōt Aaron and Moses — P^2
  2-4 3:1

Lepers, trespass and recompense — ?
  5:1-10

The suspected adultress — P^1
  5:11-31

The nazirite — P^1
  6:1-21

146

Station notice 20:22	P²
The death of Aaron 20:23-29	P¹
Station notices 21:10f.; 22:1	P²
Phinehas 25:6-19	P¹
Census 26:1-8,11-65	P¹
Identification of Dathan and Abiram 26:9f.	P²
The daughters of Zelophehad 27:1-11	?
The appointment of Joshua 27:12-23	P¹
Additional sacrificial law 28,29	P²
Statutes on annulling women's vows 30	?
The defeat of the Midianites 31	P¹
Tribal portions 32:2-15,17-38; 33:50-56; 34:36	P¹
The Stations list 33:1-49	framework document

The Book of Deuteronomy

The command to ascend Abarim 32:48-52	P²
The death of Moses 34:7-9	P¹

Works Cited

Albright, William Foxwell, *The Biblical Period from Abraham to Ezra* (New York: Harper Torchbooks, 1963).

———. "Some Remarks on the Song of Moses in Deuteronomy XXXII," *VT* 9 (1959), pp. 339-346.

———. "What Were the Cherubim?" *BAR* I (1961), pp. 95-97.

Alt, Albrecht, "Die Heimat des Deuteronomiums," *Kleine Schrifte zur Geschichte des Volkes Israel* (Munchen: C.H. Beck, 1953), pp. 255-259.

Baltzer, Klaus, *The Covenant Formulary* (Philadelphia: Fortress Press, 1971), German edition 1964.

Bertholet, Alfred, *Deuteronomium* (Leipzig: J.G.B. Mohr, 1899).

Beyerlin, W., *Origins and History of the Oldest Sinaitic Traditions* (Oxford: Basil Blackwell, 1965).

Blenkinsopp, J., "The Structure of P," *CBQ* 38 (1976), pp. 275-292.

Briggs, Charles A., *A Critical and Exegetical Commentary on the Book of Psalms, ICC* (New York: Scribners, 1906).

Bright, John, *A History of Israel* (Philadelphia: Westminister Press, 1952), 2nd edition.

———. *Jeremiah, The Anchor Bible* (Garden City: Doubleday, 1965).

Busink, Th. A., *Der Tempel von Jerusalem* (Leiden: Brill, 1970).

Carpenter, J.E. and G. Harford-Battersby, *The Hexateuch* (London: Longmans, Green, and Co., 1902), two volumes.

Cogan, Mordechai, "Israel in Exile - the View of a Josianic Historian," *JBL* 97 (1978), pp. 40-44.

Cross, Frank Moore, *Canaanite Myth and Hebrew Epic* (Cambridge: Harvard University Press, 1973).

———. "The Priestly Tabernacle," *BA* 10 (1947), pp. 45-68, reprinted in *BAR* I (1961), pp. 201-228.

———, and Freedman, D.N., *Studies in Ancient Yahwistic Poetry* (Missoula: Scholars Press, 1975).

Dahood, *Psalms, The Anchor Bible*, Vol. I (Garden City: Doubleday, 1965).

Driver, S.R., *Introduction to the Literature of the Old Testament* (Gloucester: Peter Smith, 1972), original edition 1891.

Engnell, Ivan, *A Rigid Scrutiny* (Nashville: Vanderbilt University Press, 1969).

———, ed., *Svenskt Bibliskt Uppslagsverk* (Stockholm: P.A. Norstedt and Sonor, 1962).

149

Freedman, D.N., "Divine Commitment and Human Obligation,"
    Interpretation 18 (1964), pp. 419-431.
Friedman, Richard Elliott, "The Biblical Expression *mastîr panîm*,"
    HAR 1 (1977), pp. 139-147.
Halpern, Baruch, "Toward the Antecedents of Deuteronomy,"
    (unpublished Harvard Hebrew 200 paper, 1974).
Hanson, Paul, *The Dawn of Apocalyptic* (Philadelphia: Fortress
    Press, 1975).
————. "Song of Heshbon and David's NĪR," *HTR* 61 (1968),
    pp. 297-320.
Haran Menahem, "The Priestly Image of the Tabernacle," *HUCA*
    36 (1965), pp. 191-226.
————. "Shiloh and Jerusalem: The Origin of the Priestly Tradi-
    tion in the Pentateuch," *JBL* 81 (1962), pp. 14-24.
————, *Temples and Temple Service in Ancient Israel* (Oxford:
    Oxford University Press, 1978).
Hillers, Delbert, *Treaty-Curses and the Old Testament Prophets*
    (Rome: PBI, 1964).
Hurvitz, Avi, "The Evidence of Language in Dating the Priestly
    Code," *RB* 81 (1974), pp. 24-56.
Hyatt, J.P., "Torah in the Book of Jeremiah," *JBL* 60 (1941), pp.
    381-396.
Kapelrud, A.S., "The Date of the Priestly Code," *ASTI* III (1964),
    pp. 58-64.
Kaufmann, Yehezkel, *The Religion of Israel*, trans. and ed., Moshe
    Greenberg (Chicago: University of Chicago Press, 1960),
    Hebrew edition, 1937.
Kennedy, A.R.S., "Tabernacle," *Hastings Dictionary of the Bible* IV,
    pp. 653-668.
Kselman, John, "The Poetic Background of Certain Priestly Tradi-
    tions" (Harvard Dissertation, 1971).
Levenson, Jon, "Who Inserted the Book of the Torah?" *HR* 68
    (1975), pp. 203-233.
Liver, Jacob, "Korah, Dathan, and Abiram," *Scripta Hierosolymitana*
    8 (Jerusalem: The Hebrew University, 1961).
Lohfink, Norbert, "Auslegung deuteronomischer Texte, IV," *Bibel
    und Leben* 5 (1964).
Lundbom, Jack R., "The Lawbook of the Josianic Reform," *CBQ*
    38 (1976), pp. 293-302.
McBride, Samuel Dean, "The Deuteronomic Name Theology" (Har-
    vard dissertation, 1969).
Malamat, Abraham, "The Twilight of Judah: in the Egyptian-
    Babylonian Maelstrom," *VTSup* 28 (1975), pp. 123-145.

150

McCarthy, D.J., *Treaty and Covenant*, (Rome: PBI, 1963).

McEvenue, Sean, *The Narrative Style of the Priestly Writer* (Rome, PBI, 1971).

Mendenhall, G.E., *Law and Covenant in Israel and the Ancient Near East* (Pittsburgh: The Biblical Colloquium, 1955).

————. *The Tenth Generation* (Baltimore: Johns Hopkins University Press, 1973).

Milgrom, Jacob, *Cult and Conscience*, (Leiden: E.J. Brill, 1976).

————. *Studies in Levitical Terminology*, I (Berkeley: University of California Press, 1970).

Moran, W.L., "The Literary Connection between Lev. 11:13-19 and Deut. 14:12-28," *CBQ* 28 (1966), pp. 271-277.

Mowinckel, S., *Erwägungen zur Pentateuch Quellenfrage* (Trondheim: Universitetsforlaget, 1964).

Myers, Jacob M., *Ezra/Nehemiah, The Anchor Bible* (Garden City: Doubleday, 1965).

Nicholson, E.W., *Deuteronomy and Tradition* (Philadelphia: Fortress Press, 1967).

Noth, Martin, *Exodus* (Philadelphia: Westminister Press, 1962).

————. *A History of Pentateuchal Traditions* (Englewood Cliffs, N.J.: Prentice-Hall, 1972), German edition 1948.

————. *The Laws in the Pentateuch* (Edinburgh: Oliver and Boyd, 1966).

————. *Leviticus* (Philadelphia: Westminister Press, 1965).

————. *Numbers* (Philadelphia: Westminister Press, 1968).

————. *Überlieferungsgeschichtliche Studien* (Tübingen: Max Niemeyer Verlag, 1957), original edition 1943.

Polzin, Robert, *Late Biblical Hebrew, Toward an Historical Typology of Biblical Hebrew Prose* (Missoula: Scholars Press, 1976).

Rabe, Virgil, "The Identity of the Priestly Tabernacle," *JNES* 25 (1966), pp. 132-134.

————. "The Temple as Tabernacle," (Harvard dissertation, 1963).

von Rad, Gerhard, *Deuteronomy, A Commentary* (London: SCM Press, 1966).

————. *Genesis* (Philadelphia: Westminister Press, 1961).

————. *Old Testament Theology*, (New York: Harper, 1962) two vols.

————. *Die Priesterschrift im Hexateuch* (Berlin: W. Kohlhammer, 1934).

————. *The Problem of the Hexateuch* (New York: McGraw-Hill, 1966).

————. *Studies in Deuteronomy*, Studies in Biblical Theology 9

(London: SCM Press, 1953).

Speiser, E.A., *Genesis, The Anchor Bible* (Garden City: Doubleday, 1964).

Talmon, Shemaryahu, "The Textual Study of the Bible - A New Outlook," in Frank Moore Cross and Shemaryahu Talmon, eds., *Qumran and the History of the Biblical Text* (Cambridge: Harvard University Press, 1975), pp. 321-400.

de Tillesse, G. Minette, "Sections 'tu' et sections 'vous' dans le Deutéronome," *VT* 12 (1962), pp. 29-87.

Tsevat, Matitiahu, "Studies in the Book of Samuel, III," *HUCA* 34 (1963), pp. 71-82.

Weinfeld, Moshe, "The Covenant of Grant in the Old Testament and in the Ancient Near East," *JAOS* 90 (1970), pp. 184-203.

_____. *Deuteronomy and the Deuteronomic School* (London: Oxford University Press, 1972).

_____. "Jeremiah and the Spiritual Metamorphosis of Israel," *ZAW* 88 (1976), pp. 17-56.

Wellhausen, Julius, *Prolegomena to the History of Israel* (Gloucester: Peter Smith, 1973), German edition 1883.

Wolff, Hans Walter, "Das Kerygma des deuteronomistischen Geschichtswerks," *ZAW* 73 (1961), pp. 171-186.

Wright, George Ernest, *Biblical Archeology* (Philadelphia: Westminister Press, 1962), 2nd edition.

_____. *The Book of Deuteronomy, The Interpreter's Bible*, II (New York: Abingdon Press, 1953), pp. 311-537.

_____. "The Lawsuit of God: A Form-Critical Study of Deuteronomy 32," in *Israel's Prophetic Heritage*, B. Anderson and W. Harrelson, eds. (New York: Harper, 1962).

Zevit, Ziony, "The Priestly Redaction and Interpretation of the Plague Narrative in Exodus," *JQR* 66 (1976), pp. 193-211.